THE FARMSTEADY GUIDE TO KOMBUCHA

THE FARMSTEADY GUIDE TO KOMBUCHA
BY ERICA SHEA AND STEPHEN VALAND

First Edition, 2023
Copyright © 2023 Erica Shea & Stephen Valand

ISBN: 979-8-987682-10-4

Catalog records for this book are available
from the Library of Congress.
10 9 8 7 6 5 4 3 2 1

Design & Typography by Deryck Vonn Lee
Images & Photographs by Emily Setelin
Cover Artwork by Ingrid Sanchez
Additional Illustrations by Daniel Domm

Published by FarmSteady Press in Brooklyn, New York USA
Printed in China

hello@farmsteady.com
farmsteady.com
@farmsteady

THE FARMSTEADY GUIDE TO

KOMBUCHA

Written by ERICA SHEA and STEPHEN VALAND
Designed by DERYCK VONN LEE | Photographed by EMILY SETELIN

FARMSTEADY PRESS

Contents

BLACK TEA KOMBUCHA RECIPES

TEA-FREE KOMBUCHA RECIPES

Introduction

When we started making kombucha we played
by the rules: black tea, sugar, starter, SCOBY
and nothing else until after fermentation. But
as our SCOBY replicated, cloning itself every
batch, we got a little less precious with it. What
was the harm in pulling off one layer and trying
something new?

So we started experimenting: different teas,
different sugars, no tea at all. The results were
delicious. And the deviation, freeing. We were
no longer terrified of destroying our SCOBY –
in fact, its ability to reproduce layer after layer
made us a little scared of it.

We got into a rhythm, brewing up a fresh
batch every week (or week and a day or two).
We drank it plain, drank it flat, drank it
carbonated and flavored it with whatever was
on hand. What we discovered was kombucha
was shockingly easy and super forgiving. Let it
ferment a little too long and it was more sour,
a lot too long and it was better used in salad
dressings as a replacement for vinegar.

We stopped paying attention to temperature. Pulling the water off at a near boil, letting
it cool slightly after a full boil. Dissolving
the sugar and tossing the tea in when we
remembered. In between packing lunches, or
answering emails.

We stopped paying attention to timing.
Steeping green tea for 3 minutes but also 5

or 10 or 12. We'd pass by, scoop out the bags, push out the liquid inside and toss them in the compost bin without ever having checked a clock. We understood what time and temperature were needed for a perfect cup of tea, and initially thought we should apply those same learnings to kombucha. But the results were negligible. While a cup of over-steeped tea was quickly astringent, our batches of kombucha noticeably weren't.

So we cared less about the specifics, but never about the end results. Because the kombucha we were making, in passing, muddling in whatever fresh fruit or herbs or spices we had on hand, was absolutely delicious. What we committed to memory were methods, and ratios of what worked, what always worked. In writing this book we tested and retested those methods, and these are the recipes.

What you won't find in this book is a bunch of weirdy health claims. We're still cynical New Yorkers at heart. Do we think kombucha is good for you? Generally, sure. In the way that most fermented foods are. Or in the way that a lightly caffeinated, slightly carbonated and just barely alcoholic beverage might make you feel.

Ultimately, we drink kombucha because it tastes good. We like it. And the recipes we make for kombucha taste really, really good. We hope your kombucha journey leads you to a habit, to an easy weekly routine, and to endless batches of delicious kombucha. And if science proves it does magically cure everything? Sure, we'd be into that too.

In Your Kit

GLASS FERMENTATION JAR

SCOBYs do their work at the surface. Which means every batch, no matter if your SCOBY sinks or floats or hangs out sideways, the new SCOBY will form at the surface, where the tea and air meet. And no matter what size your SCOBY is, the new SCOBY will be the exact size of the surface area. Which is to say, when making kombucha, the surface area of your fermentation vessel very much matters. Unlike other ferments where you are trying to limit exposure to oxygen, your SCOBY needs it, and lots of it. So you want a non-reactive fermentation jar with a wide mouth. We opt for a half-gallon glass version that is easy to use, easy to clean and makes just enough kombucha for us to enjoy before our next batch is ready. But you can scale (and scale any of the recipes in this book) up or down to get the amount that works for you.

COTTON CLOTH

A cotton cloth cover gives your kombucha full access to the oxygen it needs for fermentation, and provides a tight enough weave to protect it from anything else getting in. Fun patterns are just a plus. Hand wash between batches.

RUBBER BAND

While it couldn't be more basic (or essential), a rubber band will secure your cotton cloth cover to your fermentation jar. You can use a piece of twine or string in a pinch (and we certainly have), but a rubber band creates a more taut cover and use is quite literally a snap.

In Your Kitchen

SLOTTED SPOON

Used to dissolve your sugar, strain your tea bags and scoop out your flavorings, a slotted spoon is as versatile as it is essential. As it comes in contact with both unfinished and finished kombucha, you'll want to opt for a non-reactive material here.

MUDDLER

We deploy a muddler when flavoring kombucha (especially our fruit kombucha recipes). Muddling extracts fruit juices, gently crushes herbs and pushes citrus peels to release their aromatic oils. We find it to be an indispensable kitchen tool (and is great for cocktails too). The best muddlers have a little bit of give, so wood or plastic tipped stainless steel versions are great.

PEELER

Adding citrus peel to kombucha adds a ton of soft citrus flavor without any of the added acidity of including the juice. Our preferred way of incorporating citrus peel is using a vegetable peeler so that we are maximizing citrus flavor without adding any bitterness from including the pith.

FINE-MESH STRAINER

Kombucha's not the cleanest ferment. The SCOBY that turns your sweet tea into kombucha develops throughout fermentation and into bottling. And you don't necessarily want all of that culture in your glass when it's time to enjoy your kombucha. A small, non-reactive fine-mesh strainer is handy to filter your kombucha along the way.

FUNNEL

Totally necessary for sloshing liquid from one container to another (unless you have the steadiest hand ever). We like a smallish funnel (3-5″ diameter works great) that fits easily in bottles. As this comes in contact with your finished kombucha, you will want to use a plastic, stainless steel or other non-reactive funnel.

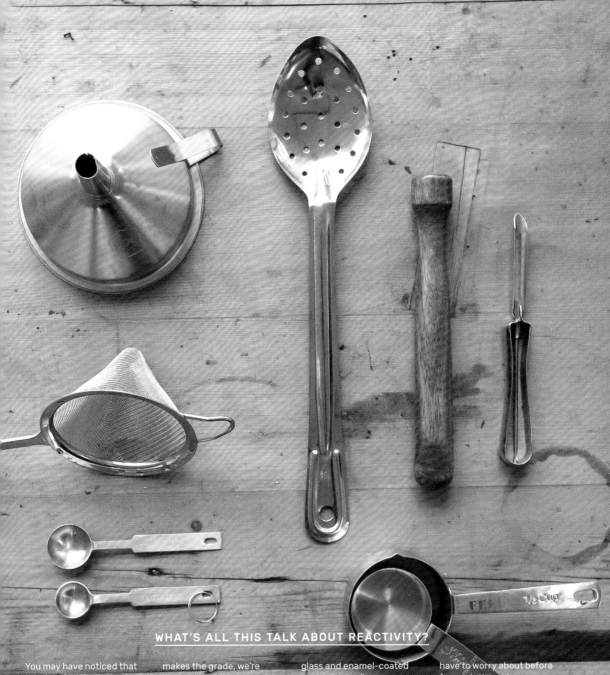

WHAT'S ALL THIS TALK ABOUT REACTIVITY?

You may have noticed that this list of equipment is downright speckled with the phrase "non-reactive." And if you are scratching your head trying to remember what exactly that means, and whether your kitchen equipment makes the grade, we're here to help.

The terms "reactive" and "non-reactive" refer to the type of material your kitchen tool is made with. Aluminum, cast iron and copper are "reactive." Stainless steel, plastic, glass and enamel-coated cookware are "non-reactive."

What they are reacting with are the acids in your kombucha, which can cause metallic flavors that you very much don't want. This isn't something you have to worry about before fermentation, when you are heating up water, dissolving sugar, or steeping your tea. But it's super important to only use non-reactive materials for anything that your SCOBY, starter liquid or finished kombucha touches.

NOT PLANNING ON CARBONATING YOUR KOMBUCHA?

Kombucha doesn't need to be carbonated. We love still kombucha and often skip the bottling step and transfer our finished kombucha into jars and into the fridge. We drink this kombucha un-carbonated and served over ice without a bit of longing for the missing bubbles. As finished kombucha is quite acidic, you will want to stick with non-reactive materials for your still kombucha as well. We opt for 16-ounce jars with plastic lids.

For Bottling

SWING-TOP BOTTLES

There are two important rules to follow when choosing a bottle for carbonating kombucha. You want a bottle that was designed to hold a carbonated beverage, and one that has a tight seal. During the secondary bottle fermentation you are looking to build up carbonation (or CO_2) to give your kombucha that delightful fizz. That means that the glass needs to be able to withstand the pressure of carbonation. And because you want that carbonation to stay inside your bottle, you need to have a good seal.

We love swing-top bottles, but make sure you are using ones that are designed to hold carbonated beverages. There are a lot of decorative bottles on the market that are made with thin glass (that could break under pressure) or poor gaskets that will let all that CO_2 seep out.

Ingredients

SCOBY

This is the culture that turns your sweet tea into kombucha. It's a little bit jellyfish-like, and its name is an acronym: Symbiotic Culture of Bacteria and Yeast. Kombucha is a mixed-culture ferment, relying both on yeast and bacteria to ferment sweet tea and add a ton of delicious flavor. That it forms into a super cool cellulose mass that clones itself every batch is a creepy bonus.

Often the SCOBY you start brewing with is not the same size as the one it will grow into. And when you drop it into your first batch (with some starter liquid) you might be concerned if it plunges to the bottom, or seems suspended haphazardly, or floats like a little country-less island not radiating the confidence you think it needs. Don't worry. Each batch, a new SCOBY forms on the surface area of your kombucha. It starts as a thin film that will thicken throughout fermentation and form new layers each batch. The top layer will always be the newest, and the bottom layers the oldest.

As you continue to brew, your SCOBY will continue to thicken, ultimately displacing would-be kombucha, which will lead you to split your SCOBY apart. Peel off these bottom layers for soon-to-be-brewer friends or the compost pile. If you want to build a refrigerated mausoleum for your retired SCOBYs in the form of a SCOBY hotel, the internet can totally tell you how. But outside of retesting recipes for this book, we've never had a need for 20 SCOBYs at the ready.

STARTER LIQUID

Your SCOBY should come packed in starter liquid. This is finished kombucha that you should add to your batch along with the SCOBY. This finished kombucha helps lower the pH of your sweet tea and kick-start your ferment. When you finish each batch, you want to remove your SCOBY and take a ½ cup of the kombucha (for a half-gallon batch) as the starter for your next batch. We recommend removing this from the top of the batch as the bottom can get a bit yeast-heavy, and you want to maintain the right bacteria-to-yeast balance.

SUGAR

Sugar is absolutely essential to kombucha. It acts as the primary source of fuel for your SCOBY in the kombucha-brewing process. During fermentation, yeast (the Y in SCOBY) converts sugar into CO_2 and ethanol. Then bacteria (the B in SCOBY) transform that ethanol into acids. This all results in a kombucha that, while brewed with a lot of sugar, isn't super sweet and is much lower in sugar than other commercial beverages like popular sodas or sports drinks.

There are many types of sugars available to you, but when it comes to brewing kombucha, we typically stick to organic cane sugar as well as plain white sugar or less refined turbinado sugar. Cane sugar provides your SCOBY with all the nutrients it can require to quickly ferment and successfully reproduce batch after batch. You'll want to avoid highly processed sugars or artificial sweeteners like stevia or high-fructose corn syrup, which may not provide everything your SCOBY needs to thrive.

WATER

Kombucha's mostly water. But you know what? So are humans. That is to say, water is important. Not important in the "let's get pH testing" way. But important in the "you just need it" sort of way. You can really go down a rabbit hole when it comes to analyzing water. (Maybe let's call it a whirlpool in this case?) But there's no need to torment yourself over water. Our general guideline is that if you like to drink your water and if you'd use it to make tea, then it'll be perfect for your kombucha. We tend to use filtered water, but if you have good tap water that works as well.

WHERE EXACTLY CAN ONE FIND A SCOBY?

The only way folks used to get their hands on a SCOBY was by finding a seasoned kombucha brewer and asking for one. However, it was more likely that someone really into kombucha would proactively gift you one. That's how we got our first SCOBY, and you might find yourself doing the same thing to unexpecting new brewers. But there are easier, more reliable methods for obtaining a SCOBY today. If you have a kombucha kit, it probably came with a SCOBY. Otherwise, you can buy a SCOBY online that will be ready to use out of the package by picking one up at farmsteady.com or another trusted source. Avoid dehydrated SCOBY suppliers. Your SCOBY should be fully hydrated and include at least a ½ cup of starter liquid.

19

Tea

The first step when making kombucha is brewing a big pot of tea. Sure, you add loads of sugar and a not-so-little jellyfish friend named SCOBY, but it all begins with making tea. Whether it's black, green, white, oolong, or herbal, tea provides the base for your kombucha. And just how these teas taste different from each other when sipping a nice cuppa, the kombuchas they make will taste totally distinct from one another too. The differences between teas will be apparent as soon you start steeping them in hot water and all the way through fermentation and into your final kombucha.

The differences will span color, flavor, bitterness and aroma. For example, black tea kombucha will typically be relatively dark in color, hearty, woodsy and rich in depth. Whereas green tea kombucha can be quite light (both in color and taste), mellow and well-suited for delicate flavor infusions. There are no hard rules about what flavors you must pair with which types of tea, and characteristics can vary quite a bit even within distinct families of tea.

We say experiment! With that said, choosing a green tea for light and delicate flavors like thyme or lavender will allow floral and herbal aromatic notes to really shine in your final kombucha. Stronger, heartier and more warming ingredients like cinnamon, vanilla or blackberries have enough flavor to stand up nicely atop a bolder black tea base.

One thing to note in case caffeine intake is something you're paying attention to, keep in mind that, just as black tea has more caffeine than green tea, the same will be true for kombucha made with either black or green tea.

BLACK

Even if tea isn't your thing, you might recognize a few major names in black tea. Darjeeling, Assam, Ceylon, English breakfast, just for starters, are some of the most common types of black tea—often named after the region where it's grown (with the exception of English breakfast, which was not cultivated on a platter of beans, bacon, sausage, eggs, mushrooms, toast and grilled tomatoes). Black tea, after it's harvested, is oxidized (think how an apple turns brown when it's cut). This leads to its darkened color as well as a woodsy, bold tea with hints of tannic bitterness—and, as a result, a robust and flavorful kombucha.

GREEN

While black tea comes mainly from India and China, green is grown primarily in Japan and China. And even though the differences in flavor are quite distinct, the two major families of tea derive from basically the same plant. Green tea just isn't oxidized after being harvested and is dried in a slightly different manner—preserving its bright green color and delicate floral aromas. This leads to a kombucha that is noticeably lighter than one made with black tea. Plus, green tea acts as the perfect base for adding loads of fun and interesting flavors to your homemade kombucha.

HERBAL

We absolutely love herbal teas, and our bodies do too. And while we steer clear of making bold health claims we can't totally verify, we absolutely rely on herbal teas to get us through our week. We brew chamomile or lavender tea when trying to relax. Lemon-ginger tea when we feel the first hint of an oncoming cold or sore throat. And peppermint tea for a late afternoon pick-me-up. Kombucha, however, doesn't have the same affinity for herbal teas as we do. It's indifferent. In order to survive and ferment batch after batch, kombucha needs tea, but specifically tea that comes from the same plant: Camellia sinensis. Herbal teas can't provide all the nutrients a growing SCOBY requires, so you can't keep a SCOBY healthy with a 100% herbal diet, but that shouldn't prevent you from brewing kombucha with herbal tea. You'll simply want to dedicate one of the SCOBYs from an earlier batch of kombucha to your new herbal tea batch. A SCOBY should have no problem fermenting a couple batches of herbal tea kombucha before getting stressed.

OOLONG

Not exactly green or black tea, oolong tea is something different. It shares characteristics, in both processing and flavor, with both green and black—but to say it simply falls somewhere in between the two isn't quite right. And as cringy as it might sound, you may be safe thinking of oolong as the fancy tea. (Just don't tell anyone we said that.) Oolong is typically a bit more expensive than most teas, and its flavor can be quite complex and varied—with flavor notes spanning the gamut from sweet and floral to woodsy and stone-fruity all the way to nutty to chocolaty. Oolong can make some truly wonderful batches of kombucha. Whether black or green, most recipes in this book can be brewed with oolong tea. But since oolong can vary so greatly, brewing with it may require specific knowledge of the exact oolong you have on hand. And if you are willing to dedicate some to your kombucha, you likely won't regret it. It'll be a tasty batch.

How to Brew

BREWING YOUR FIRST BATCH

Starting your first batch of kombucha is easy. But it's totally understandable to not exactly know where to begin. Unless you're like us, fermentation isn't an everyday thing. At its most basic level, all you're doing when making kombucha is brewing a pot of sweet tea, pouring it into a clean jar with a little more water, topping it with a SCOBY and its starter liquid, covering it, and waiting for it to ferment. The hardest part may honestly be gathering the courage to handle your SCOBY. We totally hear you on that. It's a weird and unfamiliar-looking thing that will now live on your counter. The process involved in brewing your first or second batch is ultimately the same. The biggest difference is that your first batch with a new SCOBY may take a few extra days to ferment as it awakes and gets up to speed. The steps below will guide you through your very first batch, and the recipes that follow will help you experiment and expand your kombucha brewing repertoire.

INGREDIENTS

4 Bags Black or Green Tea
½ Cup Sugar
½ Cup Kombucha Starter
1 SCOBY

DIRECTIONS

1 Bring one quart of water to just shy of a boil. Remove from heat. Add sugar, and stir until dissolved. Add tea, allowing it to steep while the water cools to room temperature. Remove tea bags.

2 Transfer liquid to half-gallon fermentation jar. Top with cool water (leaving space for starter and SCOBY). Add kombucha starter, then place SCOBY in jar. Cover jar opening with cloth, securing it with a rubber band. Let kombucha ferment at room temperature for 7-10 days.

3 When the kombucha has reached your desired levels of tartness, it is ready to drink. Using a new SCOBY can result in fermentation taking a few extra days. So if your kombucha isn't where you like it after 7-10 days, give it more time and retaste after a couple days. A SCOBY is quite resilient, so don't worry if it needs some time. When ready, gently remove SCOBY from kombucha. Reserve SCOBY and ½ cup kombucha as a starter for your next batch.

4 Fill bottles with kombucha, leaving 1″ of headspace.

At this point, you control just how bubbly your kombucha turns out. A little extra fermentation in a sealed pressure-rated bottle can make the difference between a still or sparkling glass of kombucha. The following guide will help you dial in your batch's carbonation level.

EFFERVESCENCE

STILL: Store in the fridge.
LIGHTLY FIZZED: Allow to sit for 2 more days at room temperature before transferring to the fridge.
BUBBLY: Before filling, add 1 tablespoon of sugar per 16-ounce bottle, and let sit for 2–3 days at room temperature before transferring to the fridge.

BREWING YOUR SECOND BATCH

Because your SCOBY now has a batch under its belt, your second attempt at kombucha will finish fermenting a few days faster than your first batch. Otherwise, the process remains the same, and your confidence has only grown. When reserving the SCOBY after your second batch, make sure to move the original SCOBY along with any new SCOBY that's formed to your next batch.

BREWING YOUR UMPTEENTH BATCH

You're basically a pro. You can now remove older SCOBYs as needed—giving them to friends or tossing them into your compost. We try to not have more than an inch of SCOBYs in our fermenter. They don't harm your kombucha, but they take up valuable space if you let too many accumulate.

TAKING A BREAK FROM BREWING

The best place to store a SCOBY is inside an active batch of kombucha where it can happily hang out for weeks. If you let a batch sit that long, it will be too sour to drink, but it might be perfect to use as you would a vinegar. When you're ready to continue brewing, simply use the SCOBY and the starter liquid as you would normally, and restart on your regular kombucha brewing schedule.

Flavoring Your Kombucha

Besides drinking and sharing with friends, our favorite part of brewing is getting to flavor our kombucha. There are countless ways to transform a simple green or black tea kombucha into something entirely new. A kombucha that you've never tasted before. One that's all your own.

FRUIT

Juicy, jammy, citrusy, tropical, stonefruity, bright, and downright berrylicious. All fine ways to describe the possible flavors that different fruits can contribute to a batch of kombucha. There are several methods for adding fruit to kombucha. Fruit can be steeped in the hot water prior to primary fermentation. It can be muddled and added to a jar for secondary fermentation. Or it can be added straight into the bottle during bottling. And how you treat your fruit can affect its flavor. For brighter, more vibrant notes, fruit can be added fresh or juiced. When looking for a cooked flavor like you'd taste in a pie or cobbler, you may want to consider steaming or roasting your fruit. Want to up the sticky, jamminess of fruit? Boil it down into a syrup. There's no single technique for treating any one piece of fruit.

HERBS

Herbs are like the woodwinds section of a symphony. The notes they contribute to a kombucha recipe are often light, delicate and sit gracefully atop a black or green tea base. Kombuchas flavored with nothing more than a single herb such as rosemary or thyme can be some of our favorites, but they also play really well with other ingredients like fruit, veggies, and other spices—just like when using herbs in cooking. A small amount of fresh or dried herbs can add a rich complexity to an otherwise simple batch of kombucha. But keep in mind when flavoring your next kombucha that dried herbs will be quite a bit more potent than fresh.

SPICES

The effects that spices can have on a batch of kombucha can be wide-ranging. The addition of spices can either provide hints of layered complexity, or it can totally dominate the taste profile of your kombucha with big and bold flavors. For example, adding a couple peppercorns to a half-gallon batch of kombucha will impart subtle peppery undertones, whereas a kombucha full of assertive warming spices will transport you to an autumnal hayride, pumpkin pie in one hand, cinnamon-dusted pumpkin spice latte in the other.

FLOWERS

Brewing with flowers adds gentle, pleasantly floral aromas to a kombucha. There are many options to choose from, but we love brewing with rose, lavender, chamomile, hibiscus and elder-flower. But we're not emptying bouquets by the vase into batches of kombucha. Instead, we usually brew with food-grade dried flowers. But if there's a fresh nearby flower that you absolutely love (let's say your prized lilac), and you really want to add it to your kombucha, feel free to experiment while observing safe foraging rules and making sure whatever it is you're picking is safe for human consumption.

VEGETABLES

Whether we're making sauer-kraut or experimenting with new pickle recipes, we do a lot of fermentation with veggies. And when lacto-fermenting vegeta-bles, you're using the bacteria that occurs naturally on their surfaces to kick start fermenta-tion. With kombucha, it's a bit different. Your SCOBY is still running the show, and while some fermentation is still hap-pening with the vegetables, the amount is relatively slight. The real reason you may elect to add a particular vegetable is purely for its flavor (and sometimes its color, in the case of beets). De-pending on the amount of water in a particular vegetable, it can be added to kombucha similarly to how you may add fruit—and with similar effects.

WOOD

When we talk about adding wood to kombucha (or most fermented beverages for that matter), we're generally getting at ways to mimic the effects of a barrel. Typically made from oak, barrels come in a variety of sizes and have been used for aging as well as for actual fermenta-tion. Oak dramatically softens the sharp acidity of a batch of kombucha, even adding subtle hints of vanilla. Even if you don't have the space for a barrel in your kitchen, there are still ways to add oak to your kombucha by using either food-grade oak chips or oak spirals. Oak can be charred to varying degrees, and this subtle burnt character can carry through to your kombucha. Plus, you can even soak your oak in bourbon or rum before adding to your secondary fermentation for a smooth boozy addition to your next batch.

Flavoring Methods

IN THE KETTLE

In the kettle is where you'll steep your tea. The number of flavor additions we make right here is quite minimal. Aside from tea, you might add tea-adjacent dried herbs or spices. Think lemon verbena or other popular herbal tea ingredients. This stage is really where you'll simply be focusing on making a solid base for your kombucha.

SECONDARY FERMENTATION

After a few days, your kombucha has completed primary fermentation. Then it's time to reserve your SCOBY and the starter liquid for your next batch before pouring the remainder of your kombucha into a clean jar. This marks the start of secondary fermentation, and it's the perfect time to flavor your kombucha. Or if you prefer uncarbonated, unflavored green or black tea kombucha, you can skip a secondary fermentation and simply start drinking. During secondary fermentation, your kombucha is still developing. That's why you might notice that recipes in this book that include a secondary fermentation employ a shorter primary fermentation. This keeps your kombucha from getting too sour as it ferments. Some of our favorite ingredients to add during the secondary are messy ones. That's because you should plan to strain your kombucha when it comes time to bottle. So that means muddling fruit and making a real mess in your clean, new jar before pouring your kombucha over it to cover. During your secondary, a new SCOBY may even form, and that's just fine. You'll just scoop or strain it off the surface of your kombucha when bottling.

IN THE BOTTLE

The bottle is probably the easiest place to infuse flavors into your kombucha. Here's where you may rely on fruit juices or small and neat ingredients that can easily fit into a bottle without making a mess, like dried blueberries or cut stalks of lemongrass. After infusing for a few days, your kombucha will have absorbed a ton of flavor. Plus, bottle infusions are so pretty to bring out and share with guests. An elegant sprig of rosemary gracefully hovering in a tall bottle of kombucha makes for quite the conversation piece.

How to Bottle

After 7 to 10 days, your kombucha is pleasantly tart and ready to drink. We love still kombucha and often transfer our finished kombucha into jars and then into the fridge to enjoy uncarbonated and poured over ice. But if you like your kombucha carbonated, you'll have to let it undergo a secondary fermentation in bottles to trap in all those bubbles you love.

Kombucha is a continuous process, so when you're ready to bottle one batch, you want to get started on your next. Timing-wise, it makes sense to start the tea for your next batch first (and bottle while it's cooling), but if you went straight to bottling that's okay too. Your SCOBY can hang out in its starter liquid until it's ready to be added back to the fermenter for the new batch.

WHEN TO BOTTLE

This is a great question, because it varies. When you're making kombucha, you aren't letting it ferment completely—it would get too sour and vinegar-like and wouldn't be enjoyable to drink. We recommend making a fresh batch of kombucha every 7 to 10 days for a delicious balance of sweet and tart, but the right balance for us might be a little different for you.

The longer your kombucha ferments, the more sour it will become. So if you are looking for a sweeter kombucha, bottle it earlier, and if you are looking for something more tart, bottle a little later. Your kombucha will continue fermenting (and getting more tart) while carbonating in the bottle, so take those days into account when planning what day you should bottle. Temperature also comes into account here. In warmer temperatures, your kombucha will ferment faster, and you may want to bottle sooner. Whereas in colder temperatures, fermentation may take a bit longer.

REMOVE SCOBY & STARTER LIQUID

Using clean hands, remove your SCOBY and ½ cup of kombucha starter liquid for your next batch. Store your SCOBY in the starter liquid in a non-reactive container until it's ready to go into the fermenter for your next batch.

STRAIN & TRANSFER TO BOTTLES

Using a small funnel, transfer kombucha into bottles, leaving any yeast sediment or stringy cultures in the fermenter. At this time, you may choose to add fruit, herbs, juice or other flavorings to your bottles. Leave a half inch of headspace in each bottle and close. Clean your fermenter and start your next batch.

ADDING SUGAR WHEN BOTTLING

Kombucha carbonates naturally after being bottled. When you transfer your kombucha to bottles, there is enough residual sugar and yeast to carbonate your kombucha. If you plan on adding additional sugar at bottling (like fruit or another flavoring), you will want to bottle on the later side (so there is less residual sugar), and you may want to move it to the fridge after 1 to 2 days in bottles, as it will carbonate faster. For the recipes in this book, we provide bottling instructions for still, lightly fizzed and bubbly kombucha.

CARBONATE IN BOTTLE

Store your bottled kombucha at room temperature for 1 to 3 days to carbonate. Your kombucha will carbonate faster in warmer temperatures, and if it has more sugar when bottled (either by bottling on the earlier end of fermentation or by adding additional sugar when flavoring).

STORE IN FRIDGE

Once your kombucha has reached your desired level of carbonation, move it to the fridge to store. Enjoy once fully chilled.

STORING YOUR KOMBUCHA

While you ferment your kombucha at room temperature and let it carbonate in the bottle for 1 to 3 days also at room temperature, you want to store your finished kombucha in the fridge once carbonation is established. When you bottle kombucha, there are more sugars than you want to carbonate (because a little sweetness tastes good). Moving your finished kombucha to the refrigerator to store will dramatically slow down fermentation, while if you stored your kombucha at room temperature it would keep converting additional sugars to CO_2, leading to very over-carbonated bottles.

Fermentation does not totally stop with refrigeration—just slows. That means that your kombucha will get more sour (and more fizzy) the longer it sits. New SCOBYs can also form in bottle, which is totally fine, but we like straining them out ahead of drinking if they get large enough to notice. While recommendations for when to drink kombucha vary, we think the flavor is best if consumed within three weeks.

Green Tea *kombucha is light in body, flavor and color. It's gently sweet, delicately herbaceous, floral and best described as quite pleasant.* **Kombucha** *brewed with green tea is not too sharp, and it's really easy drinking, making it the perfect base for a wide array of flavor additions.*

Green Tea

**Here's where we'd start for your
first batch of kombucha.**

This green tea kombucha is simple, both in how it's
made and how it tastes. And that's important when starting off. There
are a lot of really fun recipes in this book. Really tasty too. Don't worry.
You'll get to them. And if you're a grizzled SCOBY slinger, feel free to skip
this one... or at least read it through so you know where we're coming
from. There's another reason for starting with this recipe. If this really
is your first batch, your SCOBY might still be getting up to speed, and
you'll want to feed it a simple diet of tea and sugar while it develops into a
SCOBY ready to take on the boldest of kombucha flavors. Plus, this recipe
will give you a solid baseline for how to taste (and potentially adjust)
future batches. Let's get started.

INGREDIENTS

① 4 Bags
Green Tea

② ½ Cup
Sugar

③ ½ Cup
Kombucha Starter

④ 1
SCOBY

DIRECTIONS

1 **Bring one quart of water to just shy of a boil.** Remove from heat. Add sugar, and stir until dissolved. Add tea, allowing it to steep while the water cools to room temperature. Remove tea bags.

2 **Transfer liquid to half-gallon fermentation jar.** Top with cool water (leaving space for starter and SCOBY). Add kombucha starter, then place SCOBY in jar. Cover jar opening with cloth, securing it with a rubber band. Let kombucha ferment at room temperature for 7–10 days.

3 **When the kombucha has reached your desired level of tartness, it is ready to drink.** Gently remove SCOBY from kombucha. Reserve SCOBY and ½ cup kombucha as a starter for your next batch.

4 **Fill bottles with kombucha,** leaving 1″ of headspace.

EFFERVESCENCE

STILL: *Store in the fridge.* LIGHTLY FIZZED: *Allow to sit for 2 more days at room temperature before transferring to the fridge.* BUBBLY: *Before filling, add 1 tablespoon of sugar per 16-ounce bottle, and let sit for 2–3 days at room temperature before transferring to the fridge.*

Blueberry Lavender

In our heart of hearts, we're totally on board with lavender. It's relaxing. It just is. Kombucha flavored with lavender flowers is soft on the palate with a delicate floral aroma. If you like lavender, you'll love this simple green tea kombucha. And since lavender flowers won't impact this kombucha's color as much as we'd like, we add some dried blueberries to this recipe. They add a pleasant hint of berry sweetness, but even more importantly, the blueberries make this kombucha an unmistakably intense lavender-inspired hue.

DIRECTIONS

INGREDIENTS

4 Bags
Green Tea

½ Cup
Sugar

½ Cup
Kombucha
Starter

1
SCOBY

¼ Teaspoon
Food-Grade Dried
Lavender

10 Dried
Blueberries

1 **Bring one quart of water to just shy of a boil.** Remove from heat. Add sugar, and stir until dissolved. Add tea, allowing it to steep while the water cools to room temperature. Remove tea bags.

2 **Transfer liquid to half-gallon fermentation jar.** Top with cool water (leaving space for starter and SCOBY). Add kombucha starter, then place SCOBY in jar. Cover jar opening with cloth, securing it with a rubber band. Let kombucha ferment at room temperature for 7–10 days.

3 **When the kombucha has reached your desired level of tartness,** it is ready to drink. Gently remove SCOBY from kombucha. Reserve SCOBY and ½ cup kombucha as a starter for your next batch.

4 **To flavor the kombucha,** divide lavender and blueberries evenly between bottles. Fill bottles with kombucha, leaving 1″ of headspace.

EFFERVESCENCE

STILL: *Move to the fridge to cold infuse for 1–2 days.* LIGHTLY FIZZED: *Allow to sit for 2 more days at room temperature before transferring to the fridge.* BUBBLY: *Before filling, add 1 tablespoon of sugar per 16-ounce bottle, and let sit for 2–3 days at room temperature before transferring to the fridge.*

Ginger Lemon

An indispensable addition to every commercial kombucha maker's lineup, for good reason.

A kombucha mainstay, Ginger Lemon's status is well deserved. Both bright and invigorating, lemon and ginger play off each other so well. And even when setting aside the long-appreciated health benefits of these two essential ingredients, we love how the zesty citrus notes of the lemon sit atop the spicy warmth of ginger. We usually opt for a lighter green tea base to really showcase the ginger, but this combo works great with black tea as well.

INGREDIENTS

①

4 Bags
Green Tea

②

½ Cup
Sugar

③

½ Cup
Kombucha Starter

④

1
SCOBY

⑤

2-4 1" Pieces
of Fresh Ginger

⑥

1 Lemon,
juiced

DIRECTIONS

1 **Bring one quart of water to just shy of a boil.**
Remove from heat. Add sugar, and stir until dissolved. Add tea, allowing it to steep while the water
cools to room temperature. Remove tea bags.

2 **Transfer liquid to half-gallon fermentation jar.**
Top with cool water (leaving space for starter and
SCOBY). Add kombucha starter, then place SCOBY
in jar. Cover jar opening with cloth, securing it with
a rubber band. Let kombucha ferment at room
temperature for 7–10 days.

3 **When the kombucha has reached your
desired level of tartness,** it is ready to drink.
Gently remove SCOBY from kombucha. Reserve
SCOBY and ½ cup kombucha as a starter for
your next batch.

4 **To flavor the kombucha,** divide lemon juice and
ginger evenly between bottles. Fill bottles with
kombucha, leaving 1" of headspace

EFFERVESCENCE

STILL: *Move to the fridge to cold infuse for 1–2 days.*
LIGHTLY FIZZED: *Allow to sit for 2 more days at room
temperature before transferring to the fridge.* BUBBLY:
*Before filling, add 1 tablespoon of sugar per 16-ounce
bottle, and let sit for 2–3 days at room temperature before
transferring to the fridge.*

Strawberry Basil

We love the pairing of strawberries and basil–especially when muddled into cocktails, lemonade and, of course, kombucha.

This recipe is light and delicate. The addition of basil just hints at savory while lemon peel brightens the whole thing up, making for a refreshing summer sipper. As with most of our berry kombuchas, we recommend muddling the fruit and fermenting at room temperature for an additional two days. This gives the actual fruit a chance to ferment too, adding a more nuanced flavor.

INGREDIENTS

①

4 Bags
Green Tea

②

½ Cup
Sugar

③

½ Cup
Kombucha Starter

④

1
SCOBY

⑤

8 Strawberries,
leaves removed

⑥

6 Basil Leaves,
torn

⑦

Peel
of ½ Lemon

DIRECTIONS

1 **Bring one quart of water to just shy of a boil.**
Remove from heat. Add sugar, and stir until
dissolved. Add tea, allowing it to steep while the
water cools to room temperature. Remove tea
bags.

2 **Transfer liquid to half-gallon fermentation jar.**
Top with cool water (leaving space for starter
and SCOBY). Add kombucha starter, then
place SCOBY in jar. Cover jar opening with cloth,
securing it with a rubber band. Let kombucha ferment at room temperature for 7 days.

3 **Gently remove SCOBY from kombucha.**
Reserve SCOBY and ½ cup kombucha as a
starter for your next batch.

4 **In a clean half-gallon fermentation jar,
muddle strawberries, basil and lemon peel.**
Pour in finished kombucha and re-cover
with your cloth and rubber band. Let ferment
at room temperature an additional 2 days.
Strain out all fruit and any SCOBYs that may
have formed, then fill bottles with kombucha,
leaving 1″ of headspace.

EFFERVESCENCE

STILL: *Store in the fridge.* LIGHTLY FIZZED: *Allow to sit for 2 more days at room temperature before
transferring to the fridge.* BUBBLY: *Before filling, add 1 tablespoon of sugar per 16-ounce bottle, and let sit
for 2–3 days at room temperature before transferring to the fridge.*

Lemon Verbena

**When it comes to lemon-scented herbs
we think that, leaf for leaf, lemon verbena
is the lemoniest of them all.**

We love lemon verbena for its intense lemon zest flavor without any of the pithy bitterness that an actual lemon peel would give you. Commonly used as an herbal tea, we steep dried lemon verbena with green tea ahead of fermentation. If you have a lemon verbena plant and can harvest some fresh leaves, those are great to add when bottling for a cold infusion of lemon and herb notes.

INGREDIENTS

① 4 Bags Green Tea

② ½ Cup Sugar

③ ½ Cup Kombucha Starter

④ 1 SCOBY

⑤ 3 Tablespoons Dried Lemon Verbena

DIRECTIONS

1 **Bring one quart of water to just shy of a boil.** Remove from heat. Add sugar, and stir until dissolved. Add tea and dried lemon verbena, allowing it to steep while the water cools to room temperature. Remove tea bags and strain out lemon verbena.

2 **Transfer liquid to half-gallon fermentation jar.** Top with cool water (leaving space for starter and SCOBY). Add kombucha starter, then place SCOBY in jar. Cover jar opening with cloth, securing it with a rubber band. Let kombucha ferment at room temperature for 7–10 days.

3 **When the kombucha has reached your desired level of tartness,** it is ready to drink. Gently remove SCOBY from kombucha. Reserve SCOBY and ½ cup kombucha as a starter for your next batch.

4 **Fill bottles with kombucha,** leaving 1″ of headspace.

EFFERVESCENCE

STILL: *Store in the fridge.* LIGHTLY FIZZED: *Allow to sit for 2 more days at room temperature before transferring to the fridge.* BUBBLY: *Before filling, add 1 tablespoon of sugar per 16-ounce bottle, and let sit for 2–3 days at room temperature before transferring to the fridge.*

Elderflower

Brewed with delicate blooms of elderflower, this kombucha evokes notes of pear and lychee.

Elderflowers are the lacy white flowers of the elderberry plant, and it's with good reason they are a forager's delight. Delicate and intensely perfumed, the flowers are prized in syrups and liqueurs (like St. Germaine). The heady sweet nectar flavor of elderflowers makes for a fantastic floral kombucha. If you can harvest fresh elderflowers in bloom, do it. The season is all too short (late spring to early summer), but using a high-quality dried flower the rest of the year allows for this delicately refined kombucha to be enjoyed in any season.

INGREDIENTS

1. 4 Bags Green Tea

2. ½ Cup Sugar

3. ½ Cup Kombucha Starter

4. 1 SCOBY

5. 1-2 Large Clusters (About 6-Inch Diameter) Elderflowers, *or* ¼ Cup Dried Elderflowers

DIRECTIONS

1 **Bring one quart of water to just shy of a boil. Remove from heat.** Add sugar, and stir until dissolved. Add tea, allowing it to steep while the water cools to room temperature. Remove tea bags.

2 **Transfer liquid to half-gallon fermentation jar.** Top with cool water (leaving space for starter and SCOBY). Add kombucha starter, then place SCOBY in jar. Cover jar opening with cloth, securing it with a rubber band. Let kombucha ferment at room temperature for 7 days.

3 **Gently remove SCOBY from kombucha.** Reserve SCOBY and ½ cup kombucha as a starter for your next batch.

4 **In a clean half-gallon fermentation jar, add elderflower.** Pour in finished kombucha and re-cover with your cloth and rubber band. Let ferment at room temperature an additional 2 days. Strain out all flowers and any SCOBYs that may have formed, then fill bottles with kombucha, leaving 1″ of headspace.

EFFERVESCENCE

STILL: *Move to the fridge to cold infuse for 1–2 days.* LIGHTLY FIZZED: *Allow to sit for 2 more days at room temperature before transferring to the fridge.* BUBBLY: *Before filling, add 1 tablespoon of sugar per 16-ounce bottle, and let sit for 2–3 days at room temperature before transferring to the fridge.*

Pineapple Jalapeño

This tropical fruit–spiked kombucha recipe packs a kick from the addition of fresh jalapeño peppers.

This is definitely one of the more fun recipes you can brew—especially if you're a fan of a hot peppers. Pineapple adds some bright, lively flavors to your batch. It's both sweet and acidic, and it perfectly balances the heat from the jalapeño. While certainly not the spiciest pepper you can brew with, jalapeño is just right for kombucha because, in addition to a healthy dose of spice, it imparts a clean vegetal character that contributes to this drink's vibrancy. If this kombucha reminds you of a Pineapple Jalapeño Margarita, you're not alone. You can serve this on the rocks with a splash of mezcal or tequila for a couldn't-be-easier kombucha cocktail.

INGREDIENTS

4 Bags
Green Tea

½ Cup
Sugar

½ Cup
Kombucha Starter

1
SCOBY

2 Cups Pineapple,
Cubed

1 Jalapeño,
Sliced

DIRECTIONS

1 **Bring one quart of water to just shy of a boil.**
Remove from heat. Add sugar, and stir until
dissolved. Add tea, allowing it to steep while the
water cools to room temperature. Remove tea bags.

2 **Transfer liquid to half-gallon fermentation jar.**
Top with cool water (leaving space for starter
and SCOBY). Add kombucha starter, then
place SCOBY in jar. Cover jar opening with cloth,
securing it with a rubber band. Let kombucha
ferment at room temperature for 7 days.

3 **Gently remove SCOBY from kombucha.**
Reserve SCOBY and ½ cup kombucha as a
starter for your next batch.

4 **In a clean half-gallon fermentation jar,
muddle pineapple and jalapeño.** Pour in finished kombucha and re-cover with your cloth
and rubber band. Let ferment at room temperature an additional 2 days. Strain out all fruit
and any SCOBYs that may have formed, then fill
bottles with kombucha, leaving 1" of headspace.

EFFERVESCENCE

STILL: *Store in the fridge.* LIGHTLY FIZZED: *Allow to sit for 2 more days at room temperature
before transferring to the fridge.* BUBBLY: *Before filling, add 1 tablespoon of sugar per 16-ounce bottle,
and let sit for 2–3 days at room temperature before transferring to the fridge.*

Rose

**One of our absolute favorite
summertime garden-party kombuchas
is made with rose.**

Rose, specifically rosebuds, is a wonderful ingredient. Its flavor is restrained yet unmistakable. Floral and generally gentle in flavor, we opt to add rose to a green tea base, like we do with other softer flavors. Green tea allows for delicate flavors to stand out while preventing subtle flavors from getting overwhelmed or muddled. Adding dried rosebuds provides kombucha with both a pleasantly bouquet-worthy fragrance and a barely blush-pink hue. If you want your rose kombucha to be properly pink, adding dried cherries is the way to go.

INGREDIENTS

① 4 Bags
Green Tea

② ½ Cup
Sugar

③ ½ Cup
Kombucha Starter

④ 1
SCOBY

⑤ 6 Food-Grade
Rosebuds

⑥ 6 Dried
Cherries *(Optional)*

DIRECTIONS

1 **Bring one quart of water to just shy of a boil.** Remove from heat. Add sugar, and stir until dissolved. Add tea, allowing it to steep while the water cools to room temperature. Remove tea bags.

2 **Transfer liquid to half-gallon fermentation jar.** Top with cool water (leaving space for starter and SCOBY). Add kombucha starter, then place SCOBY in jar. Cover jar opening with cloth, securing it with a rubber band. Let kombucha ferment at room temperature for 7–10 days.

3 **When the kombucha has reached your desired level of tartness,** it is ready to drink. Gently remove SCOBY from kombucha. Reserve SCOBY and ½ cup kombucha as a starter for your next batch.

4 **To flavor the kombucha,** divide rosebuds and dried cherries (if including) evenly between bottles. Fill bottles with kombucha, leaving 1″ of headspace.

EFFERVESCENCE

STILL: *Move to the fridge to cold infuse for 1–2 days.* LIGHTLY FIZZED: *Allow to sit for 2 more days at room temperature before transferring to the fridge.* BUBBLY: *Before filling, add 1 tablespoon of sugar per 16-ounce bottle, and let sit for 2–3 days at room temperature before transferring to the fridge.*

Watermelon Sea Salt

If you were to design the perfect cookout kombucha, this would be it.

This kombucha is ever so faintly pink and speckled with just enough watermelon pulp to remind you that it's packed with actual fruit but not too much as to gross you out (or you know, get caught in your teeth). But, even blindfolded, the unmistakably juicy watermelon flavor shines brightly over a delicate green tea base, while the subtle hint of sea salt ties the whole thing together. It might just make you take a step back from the grill and say, "Oh. That's nice."

INGREDIENTS

① 4 Bags Green Tea

② ½ Cup Sugar

③ ½ Cup Kombucha Starter

④ 1 SCOBY

⑤ 2 Cups Seedless Watermelon, *Blended*

⑥ ¼ Teaspoon Sea Salt

DIRECTIONS

1 **Bring one quart of water to just shy of a boil.** Remove from heat. Add sugar, and stir until dissolved. Add tea, allowing it to steep while the water cools to room temperature. Remove tea bags.

2 **Transfer liquid to half-gallon fermentation jar.** Top with cool water (leaving space for starter and SCOBY). Add kombucha starter, then place SCOBY in jar. Cover jar opening with cloth, securing it with a rubber band. Let kombucha ferment at room temperature for 7–10 days.

3 **When the kombucha has reached your desired level of tartness,** it is ready to drink. Gently remove SCOBY from kombucha. Reserve SCOBY and ½ cup kombucha as a starter for your next batch.

4 **To flavor the kombucha,** divide watermelon and salt evenly between bottles. Fill bottles with kombucha, leaving 1″ of headspace.

EFFERVESCENCE

STILL: *Move to the fridge to cold infuse for 1–2 days.* LIGHTLY FIZZED: *Allow to sit for 2 more days at room temperature before transferring to the fridge.* BUBBLY: *Before filling, add 1 tablespoon of sugar per 16-ounce bottle, and let sit for 2–3 days at room temperature before transferring to the fridge.*

Lemongrass

Lemongrass is one of our favorite can't-quite-place-it flavors. It's lemony, without a lemon's sharp acidity, and herbaceous in a way that lemons absolutely are not. It's a flavor combination that is delicate but layered, and works beautifully in both sweet and savory pairings. Added to kombucha, it adds soft lemon and herbal notes with earthy undertones. Lemongrass is fantastic on its own or paired with berries. We love the clean grassy flavor that freshly split lemongrass stalks add, but if you can only find dried lemongrass, that will work too. However, it will add more herbal tea notes.

DIRECTIONS

INGREDIENTS

4 Bags
Green Tea

½ Cup
Sugar

½ Cup
Kombucha Starter

1 SCOBY

1 Lemongrass Stalk,
*Split and Cut Into
4" Segments*

1 **Bring one quart of water to just shy of a boil.** Remove from heat. Add sugar, and stir until dissolved. Add tea, allowing it to steep while the water cools to room temperature. Remove tea bags.

2 **Transfer liquid to half-gallon fermentation jar.** Top with cool water (leaving space for starter and SCOBY). Add kombucha starter, then place SCOBY in jar. Cover jar opening with cloth, securing it with a rubber band. Let kombucha ferment at room temperature for 7–10 days.

3 **When the kombucha has reached your desired level of tartness,** it is ready to drink. Gently remove SCOBY from kombucha. Reserve SCOBY and ½ cup kombucha as a starter for your next batch.

4 **To flavor the kombucha,** add a lemongrass stalk to each bottle. Fill bottles with kombucha, leaving 1″ of headspace.

EFFERVESCENCE

STILL: *Move to the fridge to cold infuse for 1–2 days.* LIGHTLY FIZZED: *Allow to sit for 2 more days at room temperature before transferring to the fridge.* BUBBLY: *Before filling, add 1 tablespoon of sugar per 16-ounce bottle, and let sit for 2–3 days at room temperature before transferring to the fridge.*

Raspberry Lime

**A summertime staple of Erica's
New England youth, Raspberry Lime Rickeys
pack a punch of fruity and sour fun.**

An ice cream shop favorite made with raspberry syrup, seltzer, and lime, Rickeys are a flavor pairing that works so incredibly well in kombucha. Tart and loaded with a berry-forward fruitiness, this kombucha features a bright acidity and that classic jolt of lime we expect from a Rickey. Our recipe relies on fresh fruit to seriously elevate the versions pumped out at those seasonal scoop shops.

INGREDIENTS

1
4 Bags
Green Tea

2
½ Cup
Sugar

3
½ Cup
Kombucha Starter

4
1
SCOBY

5
1 Cup
Raspberries

6
Peel
of 1 Lime

DIRECTIONS

1 **Bring one quart of water to just shy of a boil.** Remove from heat. Add sugar, and stir until dissolved. Add tea, allowing it to steep while the water cools to room temperature. Remove tea bags.

2 **Transfer liquid to half-gallon fermentation jar.** Top with cool water (leaving space for starter and SCOBY). Add kombucha starter, then place SCOBY in jar. Cover jar opening with cloth, securing it with a rubber band. Let kombucha ferment at room temperature for 7 days.

3 **Gently remove SCOBY from kombucha.** Reserve SCOBY and ½ cup kombucha as a starter for your next batch.

4 **In a clean half-gallon fermentation jar, muddle raspberries and lime peel.** Pour in finished kombucha and re-cover with your cloth and rubber band. Let ferment at room temperature an additional 2 days. Strain out all fruit and any SCOBYs that may have formed, then fill bottles with kombucha, leaving 1″ of headspace.

EFFERVESCENCE

STILL: *Store in the fridge.* LIGHTLY FIZZED: *Allow to sit for 2 more days at room temperature before transferring to the fridge.* BUBBLY: *Before filling, add 1 tablespoon of sugar per 16-ounce bottle, and let sit for 2–3 days at room temperature before transferring to the fridge.*

Hopped

Hops and fermentation is a centuries-old tale. Hops and kombucha? Not so much. That doesn't mean they don't belong together.

Beer, like kombucha, is fermented. Aside from that, however, they're quite different—from the methods of brewing to the active cultures involved to the ingredients that make them up. Kombucha is made primarily from tea and sugar. Beer comes from malted barley and hops. From piney to herbal to grassy to tropical and beyond, hops give beer a wide variety of fresh aromas. And they can do the same thing for kombucha. We like to add citrusy hops like Amarillo, Cascade, or Chinook to achieve a big fresh burst of hoppy citrus on the nose. With dozens of varietals to choose from, the world of hops is nearly endless. Want to try something other than citrus? Try one of these other hops in your kombucha: Mosaic, Galaxy, Nelson Sauvin.

INGREDIENTS

①

4 Bags
Green Tea

②

½ Cup
Sugar

③

½ Cup
Kombucha Starter

④

1
SCOBY

⑤

.1 Ounce (~4 Pellets)
Dried Hop Pellets

DIRECTIONS

1 **Bring one quart of water to just shy of a boil.** Remove from heat. Add sugar, and stir until dissolved. Add tea, allowing it to steep while the water cools to room temperature. Remove tea bags.

2 **Transfer liquid to half-gallon fermentation jar.** Top with cool water (leaving space for starter and SCOBY). Add kombucha starter, then place SCOBY in jar. Cover jar opening with cloth, securing it with a rubber band. Let kombucha ferment at room temperature for 7–10 days.

3 **When the kombucha has reached your desired level of tartness,** it is ready to drink. Gently remove SCOBY from kombucha. Reserve SCOBY and ½ cup kombucha as a starter for your next batch.

4 **To flavor the kombucha,** divide hop pellets evenly between bottles. Fill bottles with kombucha, leaving 1″ of headspace. *Note: Hops are broken down by UV light, so store these bottles in a dark place.*

EFFERVESCENCE

STILL: *Move to the fridge to cold infuse for 1–2 days.* LIGHTLY FIZZED: *Allow to sit for 2 more days at room temperature before transferring to the fridge.* BUBBLY: *Before filling, add 1 tablespoon of sugar per 16-ounce bottle, and let sit for 2–3 days at room temperature before transferring to the fridge.*

Cucumber Lime

Thanks to the addition of cucumber and lime, this freshest of kombuchas is for more than just the hottest days.

One time or another, we've all been mingling at a just-a-bit-too-warm outdoor gathering. Heading to the refreshments table, wishing we had fans, and hoping the sun would just set already, we might spot a pitcher of water infused with heavenly slices of cucumber and lime. That's the water we'd choose to fill our glasses with on a hot day, because cucumber and lime can make anything taste revitalizing. Cucumber imparts a fresh coolness, while lime gives this kombucha a bright and zesty citrus character. We love serving this kombucha with slices of cucumber and lime.

INGREDIENTS

1. 4 Bags Green Tea
2. ½ Cup Sugar
3. ½ Cup Kombucha Starter
4. 1 SCOBY
5. 1 Small Cucumber, *Cut into spears*
6. Peel of 1 Lime

DIRECTIONS

1 **Bring one quart of water to just shy of a boil.** Remove from heat. Add sugar, and stir until dissolved. Add tea, allowing it to steep while the water cools to room temperature. Remove tea bags.

2 **Transfer liquid to half-gallon fermentation jar.** Top with cool water (leaving space for starter and SCOBY). Add kombucha starter, then place SCOBY in jar. Cover jar opening with cloth, securing it with a rubber band. Let kombucha ferment at room temperature for 7–10 days.

3 **When the kombucha has reached your desired level of tartness,** it is ready to drink. Gently remove SCOBY from kombucha. Reserve SCOBY and ½ cup kombucha as a starter for your next batch.

4 **To flavor the kombucha,** divide cucumber and lime peel evenly between bottles. Fill bottles with kombucha, leaving 1″ of headspace.

EFFERVESCENCE

STILL: *Move to the fridge to cold infuse for 1–2 days. Note: Fermented cucumbers taste like fermented cucumbers, so for this recipe we only recommend a cold infusion (unless you want a pickle-flavored kombucha).*

Pineapple Turmeric

Neon yellow and unabashedly fun, the combination of pineapple and turmeric makes some of the zippiest kombucha we've ever tasted. For this recipe, we use the pantry staples of ground turmeric and canned pineapple juice, which means we can make this with literally no fresh ingredients on hand. But the result tastes anything but canned. This is one of the freshest, most liveliest kombuchas we brew. Pineapple adds sweetness with a juicy tropical acidity, while turmeric brings along not only its vivid yellow color, but also a layered, gingery and citrusy array of flavors that's balanced by a hint of earthy bitterness.

DIRECTIONS

4 Bags
Green Tea

½ Cup
Sugar

½ Cup
Kombucha Starter

1 SCOBY

½ Cup
Pineapple Juice

¼ Teaspoon
Turmeric

1 **Bring one quart of water to just shy of a boil.** Remove from heat. Add sugar, and stir until dissolved. Add tea, allowing it to steep while the water cools to room temperature. Remove tea bags.

2 **Transfer liquid to half-gallon fermentation jar.** Top with cool water (leaving space for starter and SCOBY). Add kombucha starter, then place SCOBY in jar. Cover jar opening with cloth, securing it with a rubber band. Let kombucha ferment at room temperature for 7–10 days.

3 **When the kombucha has reached your desired level of tartness,** it is ready to drink. Gently remove SCOBY from kombucha. Reserve SCOBY and ½ cup kombucha as a starter for your next batch.

4 **To flavor the kombucha,** whisk together pineapple juice and turmeric, then divide evenly between bottles. Fill bottles with kombucha, leaving 1″ of headspace.

EFFERVESCENCE

STILL: *Move to the fridge to cold infuse for 1–2 days.* LIGHTLY FIZZED: *Allow to sit for 2 more days at room temperature before transferring to the fridge.* BUBBLY: *Before filling, add 1 tablespoon of sugar per 16-ounce bottle, and let sit for 2–3 days at room temperature before transferring to the fridge.*

Mango Hot Pepper Lime

In the summer, tables pop up on corners across New York City serving fresh cut mangos dressed with cayenne and lime.

This combination of sweet, sour and heat is one of our favorites, and one we were super excited to work into a kombucha recipe. Rather than chili powder, we prefer to use whatever fresh hot peppers we have on hand. And whether it's fresh peppers or dried chili powder, we know a little bit goes a long way. When adding spice to kombucha, restraint is crucial. So we will opt for one small Thai bird chili or just a third of a habanero to bring in the fresh hot pepper flavor without overpowering heat. And that restraint pays off with a kombucha that is refreshing and layered with fantastic fruit and citrus flavor, with just enough heat to keep you drinking more.

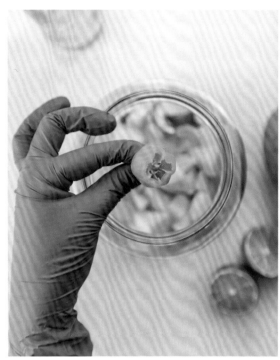

INGREDIENTS

①	②	③	④

4 Bags Green Tea	½ Cup Sugar	½ Cup Kombucha Starter	1 SCOBY

⑤	⑥	⑦
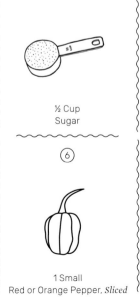		
2 Cups Mango, *Cubed*	1 Small Red or Orange Pepper, *Sliced*	Peel of 1 Lime

DIRECTIONS

1 **Bring one quart of water to just shy of a boil. Remove from heat.** Add sugar, and stir until dissolved. Add tea, allowing it to steep while the water cools to room temperature. Remove tea bags.

2 **Transfer liquid to half-gallon fermentation jar.** Top with cool water (leaving space for starter and SCOBY). Add kombucha starter, then place SCOBY in jar. Cover jar opening with cloth, securing it with a rubber band. Let kombucha ferment at room temperature for 7 days.

3 **Gently remove SCOBY from kombucha.** Reserve SCOBY and ½ cup kombucha as a starter for your next batch.

4 **In a clean half-gallon fermentation jar, muddle mango, pepper and lime peel.** Pour in finished kombucha and re-cover with your cloth and rubber band. Let ferment at room temperature an additional 2 days. Strain out all fruit and any SCOBYs that may have formed, then fill bottles with kombucha, leaving 1″ of headspace.

EFFERVESCENCE

STILL: *Store in the fridge.* LIGHTLY FIZZED: *Allow to sit for 2 more days at room temperature before transferring to the fridge.* BUBBLY: *Before filling, add 1 tablespoon of sugar per 16-ounce bottle, and let sit for 2–3 days at room temperature before transferring to the fridge.*

Rosemary Grapefruit

Rosemary is one of our favorite ingredients to simply stick into a bottle of kombucha (quite literally). On its own, rosemary makes for a delicious addition. Just ration one sprig per bottle. But if we're feeling extra ambitious, we top each bottle off with a little bit of fresh-squeezed grapefruit juice (lemon or orange work too). Rosemary quickly imparts its flavor without being overpowering, and its hardy structure means that it stays intact while it steeps, making for a kombucha fragrant with woody, herbal and citrus notes.

DIRECTIONS

INGREDIENTS

4 Bags
Green Tea

½ Cup
Sugar

½ Cup
Kombucha Starter

1
SCOBY

2-4 Sprigs
Rosemary

½ Cup
Freshly Squeezed
Grapefruit Juice

1 **Bring one quart of water to just shy of a boil.** Remove from heat. Add sugar, and stir until dissolved. Add tea, allowing it to steep while the water cools to room temperature. Remove tea bags.

2 **Transfer liquid to half-gallon fermentation jar.** Top with cool water (leaving space for starter and SCOBY). Add kombucha starter, then place SCOBY in jar. Cover jar opening with cloth, securing it with a rubber band. Let kombucha ferment at room temperature for 7–10 days.

3 **When the kombucha has reached your desired level of tartness,** it is ready to drink. Gently remove SCOBY from kombucha. Reserve SCOBY and ½ cup kombucha as a starter for your next batch.

4 **To flavor the kombucha,** divide grapefruit juice evenly between bottles. Add 1 sprig of rosemary to each bottle. Fill bottles with kombucha, leave 1″ of headspace.

EFFERVESCENCE

STILL: *Move to the fridge to cold infuse for 1–2 days.* LIGHTLY FIZZED: *Allow to sit for 2 more days at room temperature before transferring to the fridge.* BUBBLY: *Before filling, add 1 tablespoon of sugar per 16-ounce bottle, and let sit for 2–3 days at room temperature before transferring to the fridge.*

Celery

Aside from kombucha, no other beverage feels more at home in the health food aisle than green juice.

What exactly is green juice? It's juice made from any number of incredibly healthy raw fruits and veggies—most of which are green. It's refreshing, invigorating and often (but not always) pretty tasty. Personally, our favorites include ample amounts of celery. Celery is not only great for you; it tastes like it's great for you too, which gives us a healthy little psychological burst of energy. Celery lightens anything up, adding a green freshness to this green tea kombucha base. And since juicing celery can be a little messy, we steep a fresh stalk of celery in our kombucha to achieve all the tasty celery flavor of green juice without the big globs of pulp that come with it.

INGREDIENTS

① 4 Bags Green Tea

② ½ Cup Sugar

③ ½ Cup Kombucha Starter

④ 1 SCOBY

⑤ 1 Celery Stalk, *Split and Cut Into 4" Segments*

DIRECTIONS

1 **Bring one quart of water to just shy of a boil.** Remove from heat. Add sugar, and stir until dissolved. Add tea, allowing it to steep while the water cools to room temperature. Remove tea bags.

2 **Transfer liquid to half-gallon fermentation jar.** Top with cool water (leaving space for starter and SCOBY). Add kombucha starter, then place SCOBY in jar. Cover jar opening with cloth, securing it with a rubber band. Let kombucha ferment at room temperature for 7–10 days.

3 **When the kombucha has reached your desired level of tartness,** it is ready to drink. Gently remove SCOBY from kombucha. Reserve SCOBY and ½ cup kombucha as a starter for your next batch.

4 **To flavor the kombucha,** add 1–2 celery stalks to each bottle. Fill bottles with kombucha, leaving 1″ of headspace.

EFFERVESCENCE

STILL: *Move to the fridge to cold infuse for 1–2 days.* LIGHTLY FIZZED: *Allow to sit for 2 more days at room temperature before transferring to the fridge.* BUBBLY: *Before filling, add 1 tablespoon of sugar per 16-ounce bottle, and let sit for 2–3 days at room temperature before transferring to the fridge.*

Pomegranate Mint

Pomegranate, with all its bright tip-of-the-tongue juicy tartness, truly shines in this charmingly pink kombucha.

There is a fall dish made with roasted squash, feta, pomegranates and mint that we absolutely love and tend to make on repeat. This is also how a surplus of pomegranate and mint made their way into a batch of kombucha, and we couldn't be happier they did. The aspect of pomegranate that shines here is its bright, tip-of-the-tongue juicy tartness. And since, when cooking, we often end up pairing pomegranate with heartier warming spices and caramelized flavors that can sometimes muddle its brighter characteristics, we instead add fresh mint to this kombucha, which acts as a bright, herbal counterpart that is delightfully refreshing and fun.

INGREDIENTS

① 4 Bags Green Tea

② ½ Cup Sugar

③ ½ Cup Kombucha Starter

④ 1 SCOBY

⑤ 1 Cup Pomegranate Seeds

⑥ 8 Fresh Mint Leaves, *Torn*

DIRECTIONS

1 **Bring one quart of water to just shy of a boil.** Remove from heat. Add sugar, and stir until dissolved. Add tea, allowing it to steep while the water cools to room temperature. Remove tea bags.

2 **Transfer liquid to half-gallon fermentation jar.** Top with cool water (leaving space for starter and SCOBY). Add kombucha starter, then place SCOBY in jar. Cover jar opening with cloth, securing it with a rubber band. Let kombucha ferment at room temperature for 7 days.

3 **Gently remove SCOBY from kombucha.** Reserve SCOBY and ½ cup kombucha as a starter for your next batch.

4 **In a clean half-gallon fermentation jar, muddle pomegranate and mint.** Pour in finished kombucha and re-cover with your cloth and rubber band. Let ferment at room temperature an additional 2 days. Strain out all fruit and any SCOBYs that may have formed, then fill bottles with kombucha, leaving 1" of headspace.

EFFERVESCENCE

STILL: *Store in the fridge.* LIGHTLY FIZZED: *Allow to sit for 2 more days at room temperature before transferring to the fridge.* BUBBLY: *Before filling, add 1 tablespoon of sugar per 16-ounce bottle, and let sit for 2–3 days at room temperature before transferring to the fridge.*

Pink Guava Lemonade

We were first introduced to guava through Cuban pastries.

We were instantly smitten with cream cheese and guava stuffed *pastelitos de guayaba*. The guava jam inside is deliciously floral, hinting at strawberry but not strawberry, pear but not pear. We were hooked. So when we came across the fresh fruit, we were beyond excited for all our new guava projects. But when we cut it open, we were less excited to see all the pesky seeds, and understood why we had mostly encountered guava in jam form—where you can cook down the fruit and strain the seeds out. Luckily for our kombucha projects, we could mash up the guava, leave it to ferment, and then strain out the fruit while still getting all the delightful guava flavor. We love pink guavas for the light blush color—but any varietal will do. Just make sure you're using quite ripe fruit that is sweet and easy to mash.

INGREDIENTS

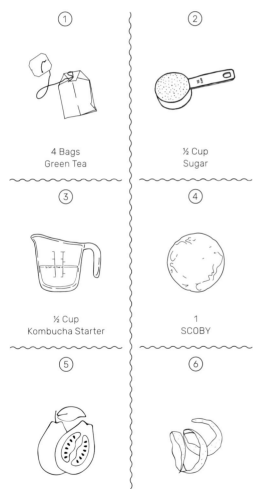

① 4 Bags
Green Tea

② ½ Cup
Sugar

③ ½ Cup
Kombucha Starter

④ 1
SCOBY

⑤ 2 Ripe Guavas,
Quartered

⑥ Peel
of 1 Lemon

DIRECTIONS

1 **Bring one quart of water to just shy of a boil.** Remove from heat. Add sugar, and stir until dissolved. Add tea, allowing it to steep while the water cools to room temperature. Remove tea bags.

2 **Transfer liquid to half-gallon fermentation jar.** Top with cool water (leaving space for starter and SCOBY). Add kombucha starter, then place SCOBY in jar. Cover jar opening with cloth, securing it with a rubber band. Let kombucha ferment at room temperature for 7 days.

3 **Gently remove SCOBY from kombucha.** Reserve SCOBY and ½ cup kombucha as a starter for your next batch.

4 **In a clean half-gallon fermentation jar, muddle guava and lemon peel.** Pour in finished kombucha and re-cover with your cloth and rubber band. Let ferment at room temperature an additional 2 days. Strain out all fruit and any SCOBYs that may have formed, then fill bottles with kombucha, leaving 1″ of headspace.

EFFERVESCENCE

STILL: *Store in the fridge.* LIGHTLY FIZZED: *Allow to sit for 2 more days at room temperature before transferring to the fridge.* BUBBLY: *Before filling, add 1 tablespoon of sugar per 16-ounce bottle, and let sit for 2–3 days at room temperature before transferring to the fridge.*

Blood Orange Sage

Sweeter and more floral than regular naval oranges, and with their deep red namesake hue, blood oranges are one of our favorite ingredients to add to kombucha. This is a recipe we lean on heavily throughout the winter, when citrus is at its absolute peak. In addition to its beautifully vivid color, freshly squeezed blood orange juice adds hints of dark berry flavor along with sweet citrus notes. We pair it with sage to balance the sharp citrus with a softer herbal and woodsy flavor.

DIRECTIONS

INGREDIENTS

4 Bags
Green Tea

½ Cup
Sugar

½ Cup
Kombucha Starter

1 Scoby

½ Cup
Fresh Squeezed
Blood Orange Juice

4 Fresh
Sage Leaves,
Torn

1 **Bring one quart of water to just shy of a boil.** Remove from heat. Add sugar, and stir until dissolved. Add tea, allowing it to steep while the water cools to room temperature. Remove tea bags.

2 **Transfer liquid to half-gallon fermentation jar.** Top with cool water (leaving space for starter and SCOBY). Add kombucha starter, then place SCOBY in jar. Cover jar opening with cloth, securing it with a rubber band. Let kombucha ferment at room temperature for 7–10 days.

3 **When the kombucha has reached your desired level of tartness,** it is ready to drink. Gently remove SCOBY from kombucha. Reserve SCOBY and ½ cup kombucha as a starter for your next batch.

4 **To flavor the kombucha,** divide sage and blood orange juice evenly between bottles. Fill bottles with kombucha, leaving 1" of headspace.

EFFERVESCENCE

STILL: *Move to the fridge to cold infuse for 1–2 days.* LIGHTLY FIZZED: *Allow to sit for 2 more days at room temperature before transferring to the fridge.* BUBBLY: *Before filling, add 1 tablespoon of sugar per 16-ounce bottle, and let sit for 2–3 days at room temperature before transferring to the fridge.*

Black Tea *kombucha is full-bodied with a rich depth of flavor. Compared to green tea* **kombucha**, *it's quite a bit darker (just like black tea itself). It's heartier with a boldness that can withstand the natural tartness that results from fermentation.*

It's the ideal base for flavors that can hold their ground in a friendly rivalry for the palate's attention. Rich, jammy fruit flavors, caramelly sugars and warming spices make for delicious additions to black tea kombucha.

Black Tea

Kombucha brewed with only black tea, sugar, a SCOBY and its starter is incredibly delicious and especially simple to make.

An essential starting point for so many recipes, brewing black tea kombucha without any flavor infusions provides your SCOBY the opportunity to quickly develop and reproduce—very important when using a new-to-you SCOBY. Plus, brewing an easy, unflavored batch allows you, the brewer, to truly taste your kombucha—without citrus, or herbs or any other flavors apart from kombucha's basic elements. This recipe might not be pushing the kombucha brewing envelope, but it'll be tasty. It'll also be the base for many recipes to come, and it might be one you return to often.

INGREDIENTS

① 4 Bags Black Tea

② ½ Cup Sugar

③ ½ Cup Kombucha Starter

④ 1 SCOBY

DIRECTIONS

1 **Bring one quart of water to just shy of a boil.** Remove from heat. Add sugar, and stir until dissolved. Add tea, allowing it to steep while the water cools to room temperature. Remove tea bags.

2 **Transfer liquid to half–gallon fermentation jar.** Top with cool water (leaving space for starter and SCOBY). Add kombucha starter, then place SCOBY in jar. Cover jar opening with cloth, securing it with a rubber band. Let kombucha ferment at room temperature for 7–10 days.

3 **When the kombucha has reached your desired level of tartness,** it is ready to drink. Gently remove SCOBY from kombucha. Reserve SCOBY and ½ cup kombucha as a starter for your next batch.

4 **Fill bottles with kombucha,** leaving 1″ of headspace.

EFFERVESCENCE

STILL: *Store in the fridge.* LIGHTLY FIZZED: *Allow to sit for 2 more days at room temperature before transferring to the fridge.* BUBBLY: *Before filling, add 1 tablespoon of sugar per 16-ounce bottle, and let sit for 2–3 days at room temperature before transferring to the fridge.*

Orange Creamsicle

Orange and vanilla is one of those flavor combinations that we feel silly for liking so much. It evokes childhood in a way that our palates apparently never intend to outgrow. Adding oak to this batch while it ferments softens the acidity, and the addition of vanilla makes this kombucha feel downright indulgent. And while you can get away with using store-bought juice here, it can veer towards astringent. So when possible, we recommend fresh-squeezed orange juice.

DIRECTIONS

INGREDIENTS

4 Bags
Black Tea

½ Cup
Sugar

½ Cup
Kombucha Starter

1 SCOBY

½ Cup
Fresh Squeezed
Orange Juice

½ Teaspoon
Vanilla Extract

Oak Spiral
(Optional)

1 **Bring one quart of water to just shy of a boil.** Remove from heat. Add sugar, and stir until dissolved. Add tea, allowing it to steep while the water cools to room temperature. Remove tea bags.

2 **Transfer liquid to half-gallon fermentation jar.** Add oak spiral, if using. Top with cool water (leaving space for starter and SCOBY). Add kombucha starter, then place SCOBY in jar. Cover jar opening with cloth, securing it with a rubber band. Let kombucha ferment at room temperature for 7–10 days.

3 **When the kombucha has reached your desired level of tartness,** it is ready to drink. Gently remove SCOBY from kombucha. Reserve SCOBY and ½ cup kombucha as a starter for your next batch.

4 **To flavor the kombucha, whisk together orange juice** and vanilla extract, then divide evenly between bottles. Fill bottles with kombucha, leaving 1″ of headspace.

EFFERVESCENCE

STILL: *Move to the fridge to cold infuse for 1–2 days.* LIGHTLY FIZZED: *Allow to sit for 2 more days at room temperature before transferring to the fridge.* BUBBLY: *Before filling, add 1 tablespoon of sugar per 16-ounce bottle, and let sit for 2–3 days at room temperature before transferring to the fridge.*

Earl Grey

**In all actuality, this is
the easiest recipe in the book.**

So easy that we almost didn't include it. Because Earl Grey
Kombucha is just swapping Earl Grey for your regular black tea. But the
thing is: it's delicious, and there is all sorts of misinformation
swirling around about how you shouldn't make Earl Grey kombucha. So
we thought it necessary to set the record straight. Earl Grey Tea is black
tea that's infused with oil from bergamot orange peels, and that teensy
bit of oil is what trips people up about whether Earl Grey works for
kombucha. And while we wouldn't recommend making an olive oil
kombucha, that little bit of oil isn't going to cause your SCOBY too much
harm. Instead, it will provide all that delicious bergamot flavor and
aroma that you love from Earl Grey tea. Feeling super rebellious?
Use it as the base for any of these black tea recipes. It'll be a secret
just between you and your SCOBY.

INGREDIENTS

① 4 Bags Earl Grey Tea

② ½ Cup Sugar

③ ½ Cup Kombucha Starter

④ 1 SCOBY

DIRECTIONS

1 **Bring one quart of water to just shy of a boil.** Remove from heat. Add sugar, and stir until dissolved. Add tea, allowing it to steep while the water cools to room temperature. Remove tea bags.

2 **Transfer liquid to half-gallon fermentation jar.** Top with cool water (leaving space for starter and SCOBY). Add kombucha starter, then place SCOBY in jar. Cover jar opening with cloth, securing it with a rubber band. Let kombucha ferment at room temperature for 7–10 days.

3 **When the kombucha has reached your desired level of tartness,** it is ready to drink. Gently remove SCOBY from kombucha. Reserve SCOBY and ½ cup kombucha as a starter for your next batch.

4 **Fill bottles with kombucha,** leaving 1″ of headspace.

EFFERVESCENCE

STILL: *Store in the fridge.* LIGHTLY FIZZED: *Allow to sit for 2 more days at room temperature before transferring to the fridge.* BUBBLY: *Before filling, add 1 tablespoon of sugar per 16-ounce bottle, and let sit for 2–3 days at room temperature before transferring to the fridge.*

Blueberry Mint

Blueberry is one of our back-pocket kombucha ingredients.

Fresh berries are available year-round, and we generally tend to have dried blueberries on hand as well. Which is to say they find their way into batches of kombucha quite often. We've dropped dried berries directly into bottles (on their own, but also in addition to lemon peel, rosemary sprigs, or fresh thyme). But when we actually plan to make a blueberry kombucha, this is the recipe we reach for. Fresh muddled blueberries and mint create a berry-forward, bracingly fresh, and delightfully purple batch of kombucha.

INGREDIENTS

4 Bags
Black Tea

½ Cup
Sugar

½ Cup
Kombucha Starter

1
SCOBY

½ Cup
Blueberries

8 Fresh Mint
Leaves, *Torn*

DIRECTIONS

1 **Bring one quart of water to just shy of a boil.** Remove from heat. Add sugar, and stir until dissolved. Add tea, allowing it to steep while the water cools to room temperature. Remove tea bags.

2 **Transfer liquid to half-gallon fermentation jar.** Top with cool water (leaving space for starter and SCOBY). Add kombucha starter, then place SCOBY in jar. Cover jar opening with cloth, securing it with a rubber band. Let kombucha ferment at room temperature for 7 days.

3 **Gently remove SCOBY from kombucha.** Reserve SCOBY and ½ cup kombucha as a starter for your next batch.

4 **In a clean half-gallon fermentation jar, muddle blueberries and mint.** Pour in finished kombucha and re-cover with your cloth and rubber band. Let ferment at room temperature an additional 2 days. Strain out all fruit and any SCOBYs that may have formed, then fill bottles with kombucha, leaving 1″ of headspace.

EFFERVESCENCE

STILL: *Store in the fridge.* LIGHTLY FIZZED: *Allow to sit for 2 more days at room temperature before transferring to the fridge.* BUBBLY: *Before filling, add 1 tablespoon of sugar per 16-ounce bottle, and let sit for 2–3 days at room temperature before transferring to the fridge.*

Coconut

**The key with coconut is restraint.
A little goes a very long way.**

Even after knowing this, our first few tries at coconut kombucha
were reminiscent of sunblock. The answer was to cut back even more,
on both the amount of coconut and the time spent in secondary
fermentation. It took retesting by degrees to get just the right balance
of coconut. That time spent among the minutiae panned out—
resulting in a kombucha that is decadent, with a gentle coconut flavor
that just hints at dessert (and not sunscreen).

INGREDIENTS

① 4 Bags
Black Tea

② ½ Cup
Sugar

③ ½ Cup
Kombucha Starter

④ 1
SCOBY

⑤ 2 Tablespoons
Coconut Flakes

DIRECTIONS

1 **Bring one quart of water to just shy of a boil.** Remove from heat. Add sugar, and stir until dissolved. Add tea, allowing it to steep while the water cools to room temperature. Remove tea bags.

2 **Transfer liquid to half-gallon fermentation jar.** Top with cool water (leaving space for starter and SCOBY). Add kombucha starter, then place SCOBY in jar. Cover jar opening with cloth, securing it with a rubber band. Let kombucha ferment at room temperature for 7 days.

3 **Gently remove SCOBY from kombucha.** Reserve SCOBY and ½ cup kombucha as a starter for your next batch.

4 **In a clean half-gallon fermentation jar, add coconut flakes.** Pour in finished kombucha and re-cover with your cloth and rubber band. Let ferment at room temperature 6-12 hours. Strain out all fruit and any SCOBYs that may have formed, then fill bottles with kombucha, leaving 1″ of headspace.

EFFERVESCENCE

STILL: *Store in the fridge.* LIGHTLY FIZZED: *Allow to sit for 2 more days at room temperature before transferring to the fridge.* BUBBLY: *Before filling, add 1 tablespoon of sugar per 16-ounce bottle, and let sit for 2–3 days at room temperature before transferring to the fridge.*

Cream Soda

**Our guilty pleasure at the soda fountain
happens to be cream soda.**

Is it a little too sweet? Yeah, of course. Is the vanilla a little much? Arguably. Is it delicious? Absolutely. And that's before we even consider adding a heaping scoop of vanilla ice cream. Once that happens, it's truly game over. It might just be the best thing ever. When attempting to capture the greatness of cream soda in kombucha form, we lean heavily on vanilla, which, once added to a batch of kombucha, fully permeates its flavor and aroma in the best way imaginable. Plus, we keep the fermentation time on this recipe intentionally short to preserve a little extra sweetness.

INGREDIENTS

① 4 Bags Black Tea

② ½ Cup Sugar

③ ½ Cup Kombucha Starter

④ 1 SCOBY

⑤ 1 Tablespoon Vanilla Extract

DIRECTIONS

1 **Bring one quart of water to just shy of a boil.** Remove from heat. Add sugar, and stir until dissolved. Add tea, allowing it to steep while the water cools to room temperature. Remove tea bags.

2 **Transfer liquid to half-gallon fermentation jar.** Top with cool water (leaving space for starter and SCOBY). Add kombucha starter, then place SCOBY in jar. Cover jar opening with cloth, securing it with a rubber band. Let kombucha ferment at room temperature for 5-7 days.

3 **When the kombucha has reached your desired level of tartness,** it is ready to drink. Gently remove SCOBY from kombucha. Reserve SCOBY and ½ cup kombucha as a starter for your next batch.

4 **To flavor the kombucha, divide vanilla extract** evenly between bottles. Fill bottles with kombucha, leaving 1″ of headspace.

EFFERVESCENCE

STILL: *Store in the fridge.* LIGHTLY FIZZED: *Allow to sit for 2 more days at room temperature before transferring to the fridge.* BUBBLY: *Before filling, add 1 tablespoon of sugar per 16-ounce bottle, and let sit for 2–3 days at room temperature before transferring to the fridge.*

Beet Ginger

Normally, if you were looking for a fermented beet drink, we'd steer you to a recipe for kvass, a fermented beverage made entirely from beets. And while kvass can be totally delicious, it is by design quite beet-y. So when we're looking for something with just a touch of beet, we whip up a batch of this beet-ginger kombucha. For beets, we recommend choosing smaller ones, as they tend to taste sweeter and less earthy. Golden beets are a bit milder and also fantastic in this recipe.

DIRECTIONS

INGREDIENTS

4 Bags
Black Tea

½ Cup
Sugar

½ Cup
Kombucha Starter

1 SCOBY

½ Cup
Grated Beet

1-Inch Knob
of Ginger,
Peeled and Smashed

1 **Bring one quart of water to just shy of a boil.** Remove from heat. Add sugar, and stir until dissolved. Add tea, allowing it to steep while the water cools to room temperature. Remove tea bags.

2 **Transfer liquid to half-gallon fermentation jar.** Top with cool water (leaving space for starter and SCOBY). Add kombucha starter, then place SCOBY in jar. Cover jar opening with cloth, securing it with a rubber band. Let kombucha ferment at room temperature for 7 days.

3 **Gently remove SCOBY from kombucha.** Reserve SCOBY and ½ cup kombucha as a starter for your next batch.

4 **In a clean half-gallon fermentation jar, add beets and ginger.** Pour in finished kombucha and re-cover with your cloth and rubber band. Let ferment at room temperature an additional 2 days. Strain out beets and ginger and any SCOBYs that may have formed, then fill bottles with kombucha, leaving 1″ of headspace.

EFFERVESCENCE

STILL: *Store in the fridge.* LIGHTLY FIZZED: *Allow to sit for 2 more days at room temperature before transferring to the fridge.* BUBBLY: *Before filling, add 1 tablespoon of sugar per 16-ounce bottle, and let sit for 2–3 days at room temperature before transferring to the fridge.*

Peach Cobbler

Combining the juiciest of peaches with maple syrup, vanilla and cloves makes for the most scrumptious kombucha you can imagine.

When peaches are in season, we often make the mistake of carting home way more than we can eat from the farmer's market. Week after week, we seemingly hoard peaches and eat as many as we can… but hardly ever do we get through all of them. Which is how peaches first made their way into our kombucha jar. And while we think that peach on its own is flavor enough (especially an in-season peach), the addition of vanilla, maple syrup and clove takes this one over the top, straight into cobbler territory. And if cobbler isn't your thing, just go with fresh peach for a kombucha that may still be your farmer's market–inspired favorite. Fresh peaches are always best, but vanilla, maple and clove make this a more forgiving fruit recipe where frozen peach or peach juice can be used without major differences in flavor, so that you can enjoy this one year-round.

INGREDIENTS

①
4 Bags
Black Tea

②
½ Cup
Sugar

③
½ Cup
Kombucha Starter

④
1
SCOBY

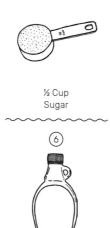

⑤
2 Peaches,
Pitted and Cubed

⑥
2 Tablespoons
Maple Syrup

⑦
3
Cloves

⑧
¼ Teaspoon
Vanilla Extract

DIRECTIONS

1 **Bring one quart of water to just shy of a boil.**
Remove from heat. Add sugar, and stir until
dissolved. Add tea, allowing it to steep while the
water cools to room temperature. Remove tea
bags.

2 **Transfer liquid to half-gallon fermentation jar.**
Top with cool water (leaving space for starter
and SCOBY). Add kombucha starter, then place
SCOBY in jar. Cover jar opening with cloth,
securing it with a rubber band. Let kombucha
ferment at room temperature for 7 days.

3 **Gently remove SCOBY from kombucha.**
Reserve SCOBY and 1/2 cup kombucha as a
starter for your next batch.

4 **In a clean half-gallon fermentation jar,
muddle peaches with vanilla, maple syrup and
cloves.** Pour in finished kombucha and re-cover
with your cloth and rubber band. Let ferment at
room temperature an additional 2 days. Strain
out all fruit and any SCOBYs that may have
formed, then fill bottles with kombucha, leaving
1″ of headspace.

EFFERVESCENCE

STILL: *Store in the fridge.* LIGHTLY FIZZED: *Allow to sit for 2 more days at room temperature
before transferring to the fridge.* BUBBLY: *Before filling, add 1 tablespoon of sugar per 16-ounce bottle,
and let sit for 2–3 days at room temperature before transferring to the fridge.*

Elderberry

Woodsy, floral and packed with dark fruit notes, elderberries impart a gorgeous purple color and rich berry flavor to your kombucha.

There are two options for adding elderberry to kombucha—mainly berries or flowers. Using the berries instead of flowers is opting for deep jammy notes over heady florals, which we like more with this black tea base. *Important: Raw elderberries are toxic and need to be cooked before consuming. If working with whole berries (fresh, frozen or dried), we recommend first making them into a syrup or tea before adding to kombucha.*

INGREDIENTS

① 4 Bags Black Tea

② ½ Cup Sugar

③ ½ Cup Kombucha Starter

④ 1 SCOBY

⑤ ¼ Cup Elderberry Syrup

DIRECTIONS

1 **Bring one quart of water to just shy of a boil. Remove from heat.** Add sugar, and stir until dissolved. Add tea, allowing it to steep while the water cools to room temperature. Remove tea bags.

2 **Transfer liquid to half–gallon fermentation jar.** Top with cool water (leaving space for starter and SCOBY). Add kombucha starter, then place SCOBY in jar. Cover jar opening with cloth, securing it with a rubber band. Let kombucha ferment at room temperature for 7–10 days.

3 **When the kombucha has reached your desired level of tartness,** it is ready to drink. Gently remove SCOBY from kombucha. Reserve SCOBY and ½ cup kombucha as a starter for your next batch.

4 **To flavor the kombucha, divide elderberry syrup** evenly between bottles. Fill bottles with kombucha, leaving 1″ of headspace.

EFFERVESCENCE

STILL: *Move to the fridge to cold infuse for 1–2 days.* LIGHTLY FIZZED: *Allow to sit for 2 more days at room temperature before transferring to the fridge.* BUBBLY: *Before filling, add ½ tablespoon of sugar per 16-ounce bottle, and let sit for 2–3 days at room temperature before transferring to the fridge.*

Cranberry Lime

Taking its cue from the classic Cape Codder cocktail, cranberry-lime kombucha is super refreshing. And given its cocktail roots, this sweet-tart kombucha makes for a fantastic mixer. Cranberries, on their own, can be a bit too puckeringly astringent to pop in your mouth like you do with other berries, but they're a perfect addition to kombucha. With their signature tart and tangy berry flavors and vibrant pink hue, they add an unmistakable essence of cranberry that harmonizes perfectly with the bright, zesty character of lime.

DIRECTIONS

INGREDIENTS

4 Bags
Black Tea

½ Cup
Sugar

½ Cup
Kombucha Starter

1 Scoby

½ Cup
Cranberry Juice

Peel
of Half a Lime

1 **Bring one quart of water to just shy of a boil.** Remove from heat. Add sugar, and stir until dissolved. Add tea, allowing it to steep while the water cools to room temperature. Remove tea bags.

2 **Transfer liquid to half-gallon fermentation jar.** Top with cool water (leaving space for starter and SCOBY). Add kombucha starter, then place SCOBY in jar. Cover jar opening with cloth, securing it with a rubber band. Let kombucha ferment at room temperature for 7–10 days.

3 **When the kombucha has reached your desired level of tartness,** it is ready to drink. Gently remove SCOBY from kombucha. Reserve SCOBY and ½ cup kombucha as a starter for your next batch.

4 **To flavor the kombucha, divide cranberry juice and lime peels evenly between bottles.** Fill bottles with kombucha, leaving 1″ of headspace.

EFFERVESCENCE

STILL: *Move to the fridge to cold infuse for 1–2 days.* LIGHTLY FIZZED: *Allow to sit for 2 more days at room temperature before transferring to the fridge.* BUBBLY: *Before filling, add ½ tablespoon of sugar per 16-ounce bottle, and let sit for 2–3 days at room temperature before transferring to the fridge.*

Blackberry Lemon Sage

This is one of our messier recipes, but it's totally worth it.

For this recipe, we muddle blackberries, lemon peels and sage in the bottom of a fermenter, pour over not-quite-finished kombucha, and let it continue fermenting for a couple days at room temperature. During this time, it's not uncommon for a new SCOBY to start forming on the surface while it attempts to bind all the flavorings together. Like we said, a little bit messy. But nothing a strainer won't fix. After those extra days of fermenting, you toss out that mess of fruit. And what you're left with is a deep purple kombucha with a jammy fruitiness and herbal and citrus notes that will make this one of your favorites.

INGREDIENTS

1

4 Bags
Black Tea

2

½ Cup
Sugar

3

½ Cup
Kombucha Starter

4

1
SCOBY

5

1 Cup
Blackberries

6

8 Sage Leaves,
Torn

7

Peel
of 1 Lemon

DIRECTIONS

1 **Bring one quart of water to just shy of a boil. Remove from heat.** Add sugar, and stir until dissolved. Add tea, allowing it to steep while the water cools to room temperature. Remove tea bags.

2 **Transfer liquid to half-gallon fermentation jar.** Top with cool water (leaving space for starter and SCOBY). Add kombucha starter, then place SCOBY in jar. Cover jar opening with cloth, securing it with a rubber band. Let kombucha ferment at room temperature for 7 days.

3 **Gently remove SCOBY from kombucha.** Reserve SCOBY and ½ cup kombucha as a starter for your next batch.

4 **In a clean half-gallon fermentation jar, muddle blackberries, lemon and sage.** Pour in finished kombucha and re-cover with your cloth and rubber band. Let ferment at room temperature an additional 2 days. Strain out all fruit and any SCOBYs that may have formed, then fill bottles with kombucha, leaving 1″ of headspace.

EFFERVESCENCE

STILL: *Store in the fridge.* LIGHTLY FIZZED: *Allow to sit for 2 more days at room temperature before transferring to the fridge.* BUBBLY: *Before filling, add 1 tablespoon of sugar per 16-ounce bottle, and let sit for 2–3 days at room temperature before transferring to the fridge.*

Pear Thyme

The savory-sweet combination of pear and thyme makes for a perfectly smooth and easy-drinking batch of kombucha.

Kombucha's known to have a little bite to it. A liveliness that makes it so singular. This kombucha, however, isn't nearly as sharp as most. In fact, it's quite mellow thanks to the addition of pear and thyme during secondary fermentation. Pear has a laid-back sweetness that we just love. Plus, thyme, with its subtly warming flavor notes, makes it the perfect companion for pear and tea. It's one of the lighter but cozier recipes that we brew on repeat. And, if you have oak on hand, we recommend adding it to the fermenter to help further soften this kombucha's acidity.

INGREDIENTS

1. 4 Bags
Black Tea

2. ½ Cup
Sugar

3. ½ Cup
Kombucha Starter

4. 1
SCOBY

5. 1 Pear,
Cubed

6. 3-4 Thyme
Sprigs

DIRECTIONS

1 **Bring one quart of water to just shy of a boil.** Remove from heat. Add sugar, and stir until dissolved. Add tea, allowing it to steep while the water cools to room temperature. Remove tea bags.

2 **Transfer liquid to half-gallon fermentation jar.** Top with cool water (leaving space for starter and SCOBY). Add kombucha starter, then place SCOBY in jar. Cover jar opening with cloth, securing it with a rubber band. Let kombucha ferment at room temperature for 7 days.

3 **Gently remove SCOBY from kombucha.** Reserve SCOBY and ½ cup kombucha as a starter for your next batch.

4 **In a clean half-gallon fermentation jar, muddle pear and thyme.** Pour in finished kombucha and re-cover with your cloth and rubber band. Let ferment at room temperature an additional 2 days. Strain out all fruit and any SCOBYs that may have formed, then fill bottles with kombucha, leaving 1″ of headspace.

EFFERVESCENCE

STILL: *Store in the fridge.* LIGHTLY FIZZED: *Allow to sit for 2 more days at room temperature before transferring to the fridge.* BUBBLY: *Before filling, add 1 tablespoon of sugar per 16-ounce bottle, and let sit for 2–3 days at room temperature before transferring to the fridge.*

Smoked Maple

Made to be savored from a tin mug while you sit by a fire, wooly socks kicked up on a log. Maybe with a few wood shavings scattered about.

Maple syrup and charred oak work together to fashion a kombucha that's both rich in color and flavor. And it would actually fit in quite nicely at the dinner table too—paired with roasted sweet potatoes or butternut squash. *Note: Want to make it a boozy smoked maple? Add a splash of rye or applejack. If it gets a little too boozy? Add additional maple syrup to taste (start with a teaspoon), stir, and enjoy hot or over ice.*

INGREDIENTS

①

4 Bags
Black Tea

②

½ Cup
Sugar

③

½ Cup
Kombucha Starter

④

1
SCOBY

⑤

¼ Cup
Maple Syrup

⑥

¼ Cup
Charred Oak Chips

DIRECTIONS

1 **Bring one quart of water to just shy of a boil.** Remove from heat. Add sugar, and stir until dissolved. Add tea, allowing it to steep while the water cools to room temperature. Remove tea bags.

2 **Transfer liquid to half-gallon fermentation jar.** Top with cool water (leaving space for starter and SCOBY). Add kombucha starter, then place SCOBY in jar. Cover jar opening with cloth, securing it with a rubber band. Let kombucha ferment at room temperature for 7 days.

3 **Gently remove SCOBY from kombucha.** Reserve SCOBY and ½ cup kombucha as a starter for your next batch.

4 **In a clean half-gallon fermentation jar, add oak chips and maple syrup.** Pour in finished kombucha and re-cover with your cloth and rubber band. Let ferment at room temperature an additional 2 days. Strain out all oak chips and any SCOBYs that may have formed, then fill bottles with kombucha, leaving 1″ of headspace.

EFFERVESCENCE

STILL: *Store in the fridge.* LIGHTLY FIZZED: *Allow to sit for 2 more days at room temperature before transferring to the fridge.* BUBBLY: *Before filling, add 1 tablespoon of sugar per 16-ounce bottle, and let sit for 2–3 days at room temperature before transferring to the fridge.*

Cherry Vanilla

This kombucha is about as close as you can get to cherry-vanilla cola. The combination of cherries with vanilla could not be more of an all-time classic. Whether it's in the countless iterations of popular name brand sodas or the timeless cherry-topped scoop of vanilla ice cream, cherry and vanilla make for a delicious pair. The rich, warming and slightly sweet vanilla aromas of this black tea kombucha sits atop a distinctly fresh cherry base, making a fizzy drink worthy of any soda fountain.

DIRECTIONS

INGREDIENTS

4 Bags
Black Tea

½ Cup
Sugar

½ Cup
Kombucha Starter

1 SCOBY

1 Cup
Pitted Cherries

½ Teaspoon
Vanilla Extract

1 **Bring one quart of water to just shy of a boil.** Remove from heat. Add sugar, and stir until dissolved. Add tea, allowing it to steep while the water cools to room temperature. Remove tea bags.

2 **Transfer liquid to half-gallon fermentation jar.** Top with cool water (leaving space for starter and SCOBY). Add kombucha starter, then place SCOBY in jar. Cover jar opening with cloth, securing it with a rubber band. Let kombucha ferment at room temperature for 7 days.

3 **Gently remove SCOBY from kombucha.** Reserve SCOBY and ½ cup kombucha as a starter for your next batch.

4 **In a clean half-gallon fermentation jar, muddle cherries and vanilla extract.** Pour in finished kombucha and re-cover with your cloth and rubber band. Let ferment at room temperature an additional 2 days. Strain out all fruit and any SCOBYs that may have formed, then fill bottles with kombucha, leaving 1″ of headspace.

EFFERVESCENCE

STILL: *Store in the fridge.* LIGHTLY FIZZED: *Allow to sit for 2 more days at room temperature before transferring to the fridge.* BUBBLY: *Before filling, add 1 tablespoon of sugar per 16-ounce bottle, and let sit for 2–3 days at room temperature before transferring to the fridge.*

Apple Cinnamon

The classic pairing of apple and cinnamon makes for a kombucha reminiscent of freshly baked cobbler.

While this kombucha might seem uniquely suited for apple-picking season, we assure it's more than acceptable to enjoy it all year round, because classic flavor combinations are classic for a reason. To achieve an apple cobbler flavor rather than a crisp, fresh apple flavor, we recommend peeling, roughly chopping and steaming your apples prior to adding to kombucha. Steaming gives apples a rich cooked flavor, similar to what you'd taste in a pie or cobbler. Want to dial this recipe from tasty-hints-of-apple-pie all the way up to indulgently-oozing-with-apple-pie-goodness? Add to your kombucha a splash of applejack with a little bit of maple syrup to taste and serve over ice.

INGREDIENTS

①	②	③	④
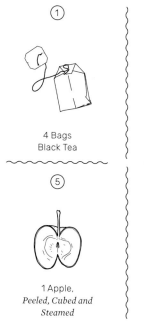			
4 Bags Black Tea	½ Cup Sugar	½ Cup Kombucha Starter	1 SCOBY

⑤	⑥	⑦	
		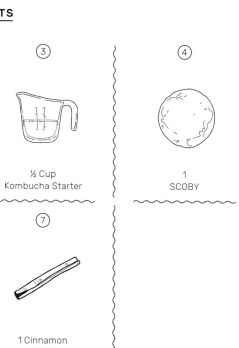	
1 Apple, *Peeled, Cubed and* *Steamed*	¼ Cup Steaming Liquid	1 Cinnamon Stick	

DIRECTIONS

1 **Bring one quart of water to just shy of a boil.** Remove from heat. Add sugar, and stir until dissolved. Add tea, allowing it to steep while the water cools to room temperature. Remove tea bags.

2 **Transfer liquid to half-gallon fermentation jar.** Top with cool water (leaving space for starter and SCOBY). Add kombucha starter, then place SCOBY in jar. Cover jar opening with cloth, securing it with a rubber band. Let kombucha ferment at room temperature for 7 days.

3 **Gently remove SCOBY from kombucha.** Reserve SCOBY and ½ cup kombucha as a starter for your next batch.

4 **In a clean half-gallon fermentation jar, add the cinnamon stick, cooled steamed apples and the steaming liquid.** Pour in finished kombucha and re-cover with your cloth and rubber band. Let ferment at room temperature an additional 2 days. Strain out fruit, cinnamon stick and any SCOBYs that may have formed, then fill bottles. with kombucha, leaving 1″ of headspace.

EFFERVESCENCE

STILL: *Store in the fridge.* LIGHTLY FIZZED: *Allow to sit for 2 more days at room temperature before transferring to the fridge.* BUBBLY: *Before filling, add 1 tablespoon of sugar per 16-ounce bottle, and let sit for 2–3 days at room temperature before transferring to the fridge.*

Licorice

**Fresh fennel and star anise partner to add
notes of licorice to this kombucha.**

There are two types of people in the world: those who love
licorice and those who despise it. If you're in second group, that's fine.
Just skip this recipe. The next one's great. You'll love it. But if you're
a true devotee of black licorice, this recipe is all you. The addition
of fresh fennel and star anise to black tea kombucha goes a long
way toward creating a bold yet balanced licorice flavor, which might
even convert a licorice skeptic in your life.

INGREDIENTS

① 4 Bags Black Tea

② ½ Cup Sugar

③ ½ Cup Kombucha Starter

④ 1 SCOBY

⑤ ½ Bulb Fresh Fennel, *sliced*

⑥ 2 Star Anise

DIRECTIONS

1 **Bring one quart of water to just shy of a boil.** Remove from heat. Add sugar, and stir until dissolved. Add tea, allowing it to steep while the water cools to room temperature. Remove tea bags.

2 **Transfer liquid to half-gallon fermentation jar.** Top with cool water (leaving space for starter and SCOBY). Add kombucha starter, then place SCOBY in jar. Cover jar opening with cloth, securing it with a rubber band. Let kombucha ferment at room temperature for 7 days.

3 **Gently remove SCOBY from kombucha.** Reserve SCOBY and ½ cup kombucha as a starter for your next batch.

4 **In a clean half-gallon fermentation jar, add fennel and star anise.** Pour in finished kombucha and re-cover with your cloth and rubber band. Let ferment at room temperature an additional 2 days. Strain out all fennel and spices and any SCOBYs that may have formed, then fill bottles with kombucha, leaving 1″ of headspace.

EFFERVESCENCE

STILL: *Store in the fridge.* LIGHTLY FIZZED: *Allow to sit for 2 more days at room temperature before transferring to the fridge.* BUBBLY: *Before filling, add 1 tablespoon of sugar per 16-ounce bottle, and let sit for 2–3 days at room temperature before transferring to the fridge.*

Orange Cardamom

Orange and cardamom are two radically different flavors that, when combined, create a well-balanced but complex batch of kombucha that's both citrusy and full of spice. The type of cardamom you use greatly affects its flavor. Black cardamom tends to be smoky, menthol-like, and with a slight charred mint flavor, while green cardamom can be a bit more delicate with layered hints of citrus. But no matter which type of cardamom you opt to use, you're guaranteed to make a kombucha with a charmingly intoxicating aroma.

DIRECTIONS

INGREDIENTS

4 Bags
Black Tea

½ Cup
Sugar

½ Cup
Kombucha Starter

1 SCOBY

3 Cardamom Pods
or
½ Teaspoon
Ground Cardamom

Peel
of 1 Orange

1　**Bring one quart of water to just shy of a boil.** Remove from heat. Add sugar, and stir until dissolved. Add tea, allowing it to steep while the water cools to room temperature. Remove tea bags.

2　**Transfer liquid to half-gallon fermentation jar.** Top with cool water (leaving space for starter and SCOBY). Add kombucha starter, then place SCOBY in jar. Cover jar opening with cloth, securing it with a rubber band. Let kombucha ferment at room temperature for 7 days.

3　**Gently remove SCOBY from kombucha.** Reserve SCOBY and ½ cup kombucha as a starter for your next batch.

4　**In a clean half-gallon fermentation jar, add cardamom and orange peels.** Pour in finished kombucha and re-cover with your cloth and rubber band. Let ferment at room temperature an additional 2 days. Strain out peels, cardamom pods and any SCOBYs that may have formed, then fill bottles with kombucha, leaving 1″ of headspace.

EFFERVESCENCE

STILL: *Store in the fridge.* LIGHTLY FIZZED: *Allow to sit for 2 more days at room temperature before transferring to the fridge.* BUBBLY: *Before filling, add 1 tablespoon of sugar per 16-ounce bottle, and let sit for 2–3 days at room temperature before transferring to the fridge.*

Pumpkin Pie

Rich with the aromas of warming spices, arguably the best pie now has a kombucha to match.

Could you make this kombucha without pumpkin? You could.
But then you'd have to call it pumpkin pie spiced kombucha and relegate
it to the ranks of all the other pumpkin-named, pumpkin-less things.
Which to us is a little less fun than the real thing. For this recipe,
mash in pumpkin puree with loads of warming spices and vanilla.
Let those flavors meld for a couple days in the fermenter before straining
and pouring into bottles. The resulting kombucha will perfectly
satisfy all your pumpkin-everything cravings, making it perfect for
pumpkin spice latte season and beyond.

INGREDIENTS

(1) 4 Bags Black Tea

(2) ½ Cup Sugar

(3) ½ Cup Kombucha Starter

(4) 1 SCOBY

(5) ½ Cup Pumpkin Puree

(6) 1 Cinnamon Stick

(7) 3 Cloves

(8) ¼ Teaspoon Ground Ginger

(9) ⅛ Teaspoon Nutmeg

(10) ¼ Teaspoon Vanilla Extract

DIRECTIONS

1 **Bring one quart of water to just shy of a boil.** Remove from heat. Add sugar, and stir until dissolved. Add tea, allowing it to steep while the water cools to room temperature. Remove tea bags.

2 **Transfer liquid to half-gallon fermentation jar.** Top with cool water (leaving space for starter and SCOBY). Add kombucha starter, then place SCOBY in jar. Cover jar opening with cloth, securing it with a rubber band. Let kombucha ferment at room temperature for 7 days.

3 **Gently remove SCOBY from kombucha.** Reserve SCOBY and ½ cup kombucha as a starter for your next batch.

4 **In a clean half-gallon fermentation jar, add pumpkin and spices.** Pour in finished kombucha, stir until well combined, and re-cover with your cloth and rubber band. Let ferment at room temperature an additional 2 days. Strain out cinnamon stick, cloves any SCOBYs that may have formed, then fill bottles with kombucha, leaving 1″ of headspace.

EFFERVESCENCE

STILL: *Store in the fridge.* LIGHTLY FIZZED: *Allow to sit for 2 more days at room temperature before transferring to the fridge.* BUBBLY: *Before filling, add 1 tablespoon of sugar per 16-ounce bottle, and let sit for 2–3 days at room temperature before transferring to the fridge.*

Chai

**Chai tea's mellow earthy notes make
it the ideal flavor profile for a soothing
glass of kombucha.**

A delicious combination of robust warming spices, we love chai in all its forms—served hot in tea or a creamy chai latte or even as a cold iced chai. Often made with spices such as cloves, cinnamon, ginger, allspice, nutmeg and cardamon, chai features a wide mix of hearty spices that stand up to a strong black tea base. And rather than simply brewing with chai tea bags, we go to the base ingredients and add an array of spices during secondary fermentation to ferment a fresh and flavorful batch of chai kombucha.

INGREDIENTS

1 — 4 Bags Black Tea

2 — ½ Cup Sugar

3 — ½ Cup Kombucha Starter

4 — 1 SCOBY

5 — 4 Cloves

6 — 2 Pieces Candied Ginger

7 — ½ Teaspoon Cardamom

8 — ¼ Teaspoon Allspice

9 — 1 Cinnamon Stick

10 — ¼ Teaspoon Vanilla Extract

DIRECTIONS

1 **Bring one quart of water to just shy of a boil.** Remove from heat. Add sugar, and stir until dissolved. Add tea, allowing it to steep while the water cools to room temperature. Remove tea bags.

2 **Transfer liquid to half-gallon fermentation jar.** Top with cool water (leaving space for starter and SCOBY). Add kombucha starter, then place SCOBY in jar. Cover jar opening with cloth, securing it with a rubber band. Let kombucha ferment at room temperature for 7 days.

3 **Gently remove SCOBY from kombucha.** Reserve SCOBY and ½ cup kombucha as a starter for your next batch.

4 **In a clean half-gallon fermentation jar, add all spices.** Pour in finished kombucha and re-cover with your cloth and rubber band. Let ferment at room temperature an additional 2 days. Strain out spices and any SCOBYs that may have formed, then fill bottles with kombucha, leaving 1″ of headspace.

EFFERVESCENCE

STILL: *Store in the fridge.* LIGHTLY FIZZED: *Allow to sit for 2 more days at room temperature before transferring to the fridge.* BUBBLY: *Before filling, add 1 tablespoon of sugar per 16-ounce bottle, and let sit for 2–3 days at room temperature before transferring to the fridge.*

Tea-free *kombucha? How can it be? Kombucha is literally fermented tea. For us, if we are using a SCOBY (instead of a ginger bug or wild yeast like we do for natural sodas), we consider it a kombucha. And while we can totally see how purists might disagree with what these recipes should be called, there* is no denying they are delicious. We strongly recommend keeping your regular **kombucha** going alongside any of these recipes (it would stress the culture to change up its food source every week). But if you have SCOBYs to spare, peel off a layer and make one of these tangy, tea-free kombuchas your next batch.

Chamomile

We love the delicate, calming floral character of chamomile. It's one of our favorite teas to sip, and one that we absolutely wanted to add to kombucha. And while stronger florals like rose and lavender work great with a green tea base, for chamomile it just doesn't do. So instead of settling for a hybrid tea and chamomile approach, we ditched the tea all together and went with a 100% chamomile batch. This kombucha is super light, floral and refreshing. We drink it straight, or carbonated with a little honey.

DIRECTIONS

INGREDIENTS

1 Cup
Dried Chamomile

½ Cup
Sugar

½ Cup
Kombucha Starter,
*(preferably green tea
kombucha)*

1 SCOBY

1 **Bring one quart of water to just shy of a boil.** Remove from heat. Add sugar, and stir until dissolved. Add chamomile and steep for 10 minutes. Remove chamomile and let liquid cool to room temperature.

2 **Transfer liquid to half–gallon fermentation jar.** Top with cool water (leaving space for starter and SCOBY). Add kombucha starter, then place SCOBY in jar. Cover jar opening with cloth, securing it with a rubber band. Let kombucha ferment at room temperature for 7–10 days.

3 **When the kombucha has reached your desired levels of tartness**, it is ready to drink. Remove SCOBY from kombucha and discard.

4 **Fill bottles with kombucha**, leaving 1″ of headspace.

EFFERVESCENCE

STILL: *Store in the fridge.*

LIGHTLY FIZZED: *Allow to sit for 2 more days at room temperature before transferring to the fridge.*

BUBBLY: *Before filling, add 1 tablespoon of sugar per 16-ounce bottle, and let sit for 2–3 days at room temperature before transferring to the fridge.*

Hibiscus

What this recipe lacks in tea, it makes up for with a head-turning pink glow and bold tropical flavors that don't hold back.

Hibiscus kombucha is a delight. It's a vivid hot pink—even turning SCOBYs a bright pink too! It's quite different from most kombuchas you've made (or likely tasted). Rather than being brewed and fermented with green or black tea, it's made entirely with dried hibiscus flowers. Exotically floral and fruity with a deep magenta hue, hibiscus's bright and sour characteristics are truly elevated by this kombucha. And although its flavor is totally unique, hibiscus, in kombucha form, imparts notes of cranberry as well as other more tropically tart tones. This is a recipe we come back to often, all the while keeping at least one tea-based kombucha batch going so that we never run out of strong, healthy SCOBYs.

INGREDIENTS

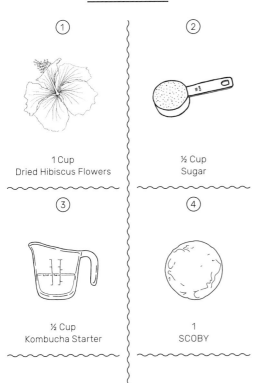

①

1 Cup
Dried Hibiscus Flowers

②

½ Cup
Sugar

③

½ Cup
Kombucha Starter

④

1
SCOBY

1 **Bring one quart of water to just shy of a boil.** Remove from heat. Add sugar, and stir until dissolved. Add hibiscus, allowing it to steep while the water cools to room temperature. Remove hibiscus.

2 **Transfer liquid to half-gallon fermentation jar.** Top with cool water (leaving space for starter and SCOBY). Add kombucha starter, then place SCOBY in jar. Cover jar opening with cloth, securing it with a rubber band. Let kombucha ferment at room temperature for 7–10 days.

3 **When the kombucha has reached your desired levels of tartness**, it is ready to drink. Remove SCOBY from kombucha and discard.

4 **Fill bottles with kombucha**, leaving 1″ of headspace.

EFFERVESCENCE

STILL: *Store in the fridge.*

LIGHTLY FIZZED: *Allow to sit for 2 more days at room temperature before transferring to the fridge.*

BUBBLY: *Before filling, add 1 tablespoon of sugar per 16-ounce bottle, and let sit for 2–3 days at room temperature before transferring to the fridge.*

Coffee

**We like our coffee black and
our kombucha, in this tea-free recipe,
brewed with a whole lot of coffee.**

When we first heard about coffee kombucha, we actively cringed. We love kombucha, but we love, love coffee in a need-to-know bean origin, roast details, third wave coffee sort of way. We dial in our grind, and we use our gram scale daily—it's actually a jewelry scale that works quite nicely for coffee. No judgement, but as a rule, we reject all unnecessary flavorings and even most preparations using milk. We love coffee as coffee, kombucha as kombucha, and really thought the two ought not be combined. Then we looked into different methods people were using to make coffee kombucha, which immediately made us think: Eek, that's not how we would make it. Which obviously meant we then had to perfect our version of coffee kombucha. Here it is.

INGREDIENTS

① 1 ⅓ Cup (120 Grams)
Coffee, *Ground*

② ½ Cup
Sugar

③ ½ Cup
Kombucha Starter

④ 1
SCOBY

DIRECTIONS

1 **Steep coffee in one quart of water at room temperature overnight.** Strain and discard coffee grounds. Add sugar and whisk vigorously until dissolved.

2 **Transfer liquid to half-gallon fermentation jar.** Top with cool water (leaving space for starter and SCOBY). Add kombucha starter, then place SCOBY in jar. Cover jar opening with cloth, securing it with a rubber band. Let kombucha ferment at room temperature for 7–10 days.

3 **When the kombucha has reached your desired levels of tartness**, it is ready to drink. Remove SCOBY from kombucha and discard.

4 **Fill bottles with kombucha**, leaving 1″ of headspace.

EFFERVESCENCE

STILL: *Store in the fridge.* LIGHTLY FIZZED: *Allow to sit for 2 more days at room temperature before transferring to the fridge.* BUBBLY: *Before filling, add 1 tablespoon of sugar per 16-ounce bottle, and let sit for 2–3 days at room temperature before transferring to the fridge.*

Concord Grape

**The juiciest, most grape-iest kombucha
you can imagine is brewed not with tea, but with
cups of fresh, in-season concord grapes.**

This kombucha has some of the best grape flavors you will
find in any beverage—not just kombucha. If you like fresh and in-season
concord grapes, you'll absolutely love this recipe. We look forward to
the few weeks every year when we can find local concord grapes at the
farmers market. At our nearby market, the juiciest grapes are always
swarmed with honeybees who just know how tasty they are. Admittedly,
the bees can be a little scary for some, but they're a great sign for us.
Those are the grapes we pick up to make a few batches of tea-free concord
grape kombucha to share with friends all season long.

INGREDIENTS

①

1 Quart
Concord Grapes,
Stems Removed

②

½ Cup
Sugar

③

½ Cup
Kombucha Starter

④

1
SCOBY

DIRECTIONS

1 **Bring one quart of water to just shy of a boil.** Remove from heat. Add sugar, and stir until dissolved. Add concord grapes, allowing them to burst while the water cools to room temperature.

2 **Transfer liquid (including grapes) to half-gallon fermentation jar.** Top with cool water (leaving space for starter and SCOBY). Add kombucha starter, then place SCOBY in jar. Cover jar opening with cloth, securing it with a rubber band. Let kombucha ferment at room temperature for 7–10 days.

3 **When the kombucha has reached your desired levels of tartness,** it is ready to drink. Remove SCOBY and grapes from kombucha and discard.

4 **Fill bottles with kombucha**, leaving 1″ of headspace.

EFFERVESCENCE

STILL: *Store in the fridge.*

LIGHTLY FIZZED: *Allow to sit for 2 more days at room temperature before transferring to the fridge.*

BUBBLY: *Before filling, add 1 tablespoon of sugar per 16-ounce bottle, and let sit for 2–3 days at room temperature before transferring to the fridge.*

Blueberry

**Loads of blueberries make this
kombucha the deepest blue and the most
berry-filled drink imaginable.**

Brewing a batch of blueberry kombucha is a special treat for us. When we see fresh, local blueberries at the farmers market for the first time in a season, we always grab an extra basket to reserve for kombucha. Few things compare to kombucha brewed exclusively with blueberries. Juicy and overflowing with real blueberry flavor, it's always a true delight. That unmistakable blueberry flavor carries through all the way from the farmers market to the finished kombucha. It's delicious, vibrantly blue and an absolute pure distillation of everything worth loving about blueberries. But since local blueberries are not always in season and can get a little pricey, we also wait for a sale at the fruit stand. If there's a good deal on blueberries to be had, we're making this kombucha without fail.

INGREDIENTS

①

3 Cups
Blueberries

②

½ Cup
Sugar

③

½ Cup
Kombucha Starter

④

1
SCOBY

DIRECTIONS

1 **Bring one quart of water to just shy of a boil.** Remove from heat. Add sugar, and stir until dissolved. Add blueberries, allowing them to burst while the water cools to room temperature.

2 **Transfer liquid (including blueberries) to half–gallon fermentation jar**. Top with cool water (leaving space for starter and SCOBY). Add kombucha starter, then place SCOBY in jar. Cover jar opening with cloth, securing it with a rubber band. Let kombucha ferment at room temperature for 7–10 days.

3 **When the kombucha has reached your desired levels of tartness**, it is ready to drink. Remove SCOBY and blueberries from kombucha and discard.

4 **Fill bottles with kombucha**, leaving 1″ of headspace.

EFFERVESCENCE

STILL: *Store in the fridge.*

LIGHTLY FIZZED: *Allow to sit for 2 more days at room temperature before transferring to the fridge.*

BUBBLY: *Before filling, add 1 tablespoon of sugar per 16-ounce bottle, and let sit for 2–3 days at room temperature before transferring to the fridge.*

Index

For Lovers of All Things Handmade. For devotees of great food made simply. For fans of getting their hands dirty. *For the curious.* For would-be know-it-alls and practicing scientists. For chefs. *For followers of recipes and creators of new ones.* For those who wing it. For keepers of window boxes and curators of raised beds. For weekend believers. *For rooftop, urban and backyard farmers.* For those taking their crush on farming to the next level, *There's Farmsteady.*